> the **2 degree** difference

John Trent

> the **2 degree** difference

how little things can **change** everything

PUBLISHING GROUP
Nashville, Tennessee

Ten-digit ISBN: 0-8054-3064-4
Thirteen-digit ISBN: 978-0-8054-3064-6

Published by B&H Publishing Group,
Nashville, Tennessee

Dewey Decimal Classification: 248.84
Subject Heading: CHRISTIAN LIFE \ DISCIPLESHIP \
WORK ENVIRONMENT

Unless otherwise stated, Scripture quotations are from the NASB, New
American Standard Bible, © the Lockman Foundation, 1960, 1962, 1963,
1968, 1971, 1972, 1973, 1975, 1977, 1995; used by permission.

Other version used: *The Message,* the New Testament in Contemporary
English, © 1993 by Eugene H. Peterson, published by NavPress,
Colorado Springs, Colo.

1 2 3 4 5 6 7 8 9 10   10 09 08 07 06

contents

2°

2°

dedication

have had the great honor in the past of dedicating books to my beloved wife, Cindy, and each of our daughters, Kari and Laura. However, our entire family is in agreement that this book should be dedicated to my two brothers, Joe and Jeff. Certainly it's for their long-suffering patience in putting up with an "Otter" for a brother, but it's also for being the kind of "always there for you" brothers that most people only wish they could have. Each brother has been an incredible support all my life, willing to help in large ways and small, and a tremendous blessing. You'll soon read about an outstanding friend named "Eric" who figures prominently in this book. I have two Erics in my life, my brothers Joe and Jeff. I love and appreciate you both. Your brother, John.

2°

acknowledgments

Very special thanks to Len Goss and the entire team of professionals at B&H Publishing Group. Thanks are in order too to Darrell Heringer, outstanding ministry volunteer and closest of friends, for his taking on extra burdens to free me for the writing of this book. Thanks go out as well to Jim McGuire, Doug Childress, and Bob Leenhouts, committed board members and lifelong brothers in Christ, ministry, and life. Tony Wheeler, soon to be Dr. Tony Wheeler, family pastor extraordinaire at Highlands Church in Scottsdale, Arizona. Tony deserves special thanks for helping me teach the initial classes at The Center for StrongFamilies about *The 2 Degree Difference*. And finally, thanks are due to our very first alpha group at The Center for StrongFamilies. The following people were incredibly patient as Tony and I piloted with them in rough form what would become our core curriculum at the Center, including many of the ideas found in this book.

Chris and Deborah Berry
Wes and Kristen Buchanan

2°

Jeff and Lorri Bucholz
Marlene Daniels
Julie Hallmark
Dan and Angela Mazzola
Scott and Sherry Mckown
Chad and Kathy Merwin
Shawn and Dani Meyer
Rob and Nicole Scrivo
Stephanie Stewart
Casey and Jennifer Wolf

the starting place for too many purposeful people

ecause you're reading these words, I know you're busy, committed, and frustrated. No, I'm not a mind reader. But I do travel across the country extensively. (I've accumulated almost three million frequent-flyer miles on American Airlines alone, all on domestic flights.) In the past decade, as I've dropped in on people in large cities and small towns across America, I have been privileged to meet literally hundreds of men and women who desire, often more than anything, to have a life that really counts. Nationally they're part of the millions of people who personally, in their workplace, family, *and* spiritual life, want to lie down at night knowing they've spent a full day living a life of purpose and significance. Yet an amazingly high number of these same highly committed, highly caring people actually wake up in the morning feeling incredibly frustrated. They've prayed and planned; they've read books and gone to seminars; they've attended every focus group at work and small-group meeting at their church, faithfully filled out every handout they were given, and *still* they feel like their life is stuck at the starting line.

Still, after all that effort, too many committed people simply don't seem to be moving forward. In fact, many feel like they're sliding backwards as others their same age or in a similar situation disappear ahead of them, people who seem to know or have something they don't. A verse in the book of Proverbs reads, "Hope deferred makes the heart sick" (Proverbs 13:12). Being heartsick from dashed expectations for change describes the state of many of the people I meet, and it's a key reason for writing this book.

These wonderful, intelligent, dedicated, purpose-focused people I've met have no lack of "want to" when it comes to change. But in their heart of hearts, they know things simply aren't changing right now; and for many people change *does* need to happen—*now.*

You'll meet one such person in this book.

In a short time you'll read the story of Brian, who woke up one day and—despite all the planning, all the praying, all the workplace seminars and weekend conferences, all the church services and heartfelt commitments that things would be different—his life didn't seem to move one inch in a truly purposeful direction. The life he always wanted, his best life now, bore no resemblance to the life he really lived. Not really. And as the days turned into months and then pushed on into years, Brian could have been selected as the poster child for what it means to be heartsick.

But here's the good news.

In the short time it will take you to read this story, perhaps on a cross-country plane flight or over a single uninterrupted evening, you'll discover a small, incredibly powerful principle. It's a tool as solid as Scripture, almost universally overlooked in our day, that can help people like Brian—*and you*—actually take those crucial steps toward real change.

Does that mean all the work people have done in writing down and planning out a life of purpose and significance is somehow misguided or unimportant? Absolutely not! If anything, focusing on getting a clear purpose is incredibly helpful. You should read *The Purpose-Driven Life* and other recent books like it that provide tremendous encouragement and inspiration. Putting time into planning out a life of purpose is like building a car, part by important part. But after all the labor to piece together what a life of purpose and significance looks like, most people still leave out one small but important item—a tiny ignition switch that is essential to get that car moving!

In this story you'll discover how one man found that small key to change, the same one you'll soon be able to add to your life as well. It's something that can get your life moving, whether you're deeply heartsick or just mildly frustrated. It has been a key for many people, like you, to finally see real movement in their career, their home, their health, and even their heart for God.

In a few pages you'll be introduced to this powerful, scriptural, catalytic tool for change. So whether you're an overwhelmed mom of young kids or teenagers, a time-strapped college student, a businessperson needing to get out of a workplace rut, or even the pastor of a growing congregation wanting to raise the spiritual bar for your entire congregation, it's time to learn about the *2 Degree Difference*. It's time to learn how the small marks you make in the margins of your life today can make all the difference in boldly living out a life of purpose and significance both today and tomorrow.

And once you learn this tool, it can become a wonderful gift to share with your frustrated family and friends as well.

John Trent, Ph.D.
President, The Center for StrongFamilies
and StrongFamilies.com

Part I

2°

a story of hope realized
and a life of purpose lived out

waking up to an unwanted reality

B rian's story began long ago and far, far away . . .

The dirt road that served as Main Street was nearly empty of people now. Even the old hound that was a fixture in front of the town's general store had finally wandered back into town. He was sprawled out, occupying his usual place in the shade. That's when the door to the sheriff's office opened slowly, and the tall man in the black suit stepped outside.

As quiet as a moving shadow, he shut the wooden door behind him, his eyes darting quickly left, then right, then left again, reflecting hard-learned habits of a careful man. Satisfied there was nothing unusual to be seen, he relaxed slightly as he stood on the wooden sidewalk, looking north toward the stables and rail station at the far end of the street. It may have been the only street of this town, but it was his town. And after what had happened just a few hours earlier, it really was *his* town now.

Earlier that afternoon the daily supply train had whistled to a stop. Emerging out of the cloud of steam thrown up by the loco-motive's huge wood-fired engine had come a huddle of Polish immi-grants in decidedly European clothing; a balding conductor carrying a single, zippered-sack of mail; a tall, rail-thin porter pushing a cart filled with at least a dozen odd-sized boxes destined for the general store; and death.

2°

Death stepped off the train that day in the form of Rustin Lewis and the Barker brothers, hard cases all. Each man carried a Colt .44 revolver, holstered low and tied down in the gunfighter way. The two brothers each wore belts of ammunition that crossed their chests and had an extra pistol stuffed in their belts. In addition to his sidearm, Lewis had brought his favorite killing weapon, a cut-down 12-gauge shotgun, both barrels loaded with buckshot, his pockets filled with extra ammunition.

They were there to kill the sheriff, the only man who had ever bested them.

A few years ago this sheriff had led a posse against them. For four days, until their trail played out and finally went stone cold, the posse had dogged these same bandits over rough, dry land. Finally, the posse had reluctantly given up and turned back to town—but not their sheriff. He had refused to give up and had gone on alone, at one point tracking the outlaws ahead of him over solid rock for the better part of a day. At dawn on his sixth day out of town, he surprised them, capturing all three men without having to fire a single shot.

A month later at their trial, the circuit judge who had traveled to town, sentenced each man in turn to four years of hard labor in the Yuma Territorial Prison. *Hard labor.* It had been all of that, all right. Four long, brutally hard years of breaking rocks and many of the prisoners' wills as well. Not for these three however. Every day in the scorching Arizona sun, as these three convicts slammed down a pick or shovel, they had seen that sheriff's face in the rock or rock-hard dirt before them. In the evenings as they huddled in their cells, they had dreamed and planned of nothing else than killing the one man most responsible for putting them behind bars. And after this man was dead, then they'd see to it that the two-bit town he guarded would die along with him—payment for their sending a posse out after them in the first place.

But first things first. According to their plan, the dying would start with that tall lawman with the steady, slate-grey eyes.

As the sheriff stood on the sidewalk, thumbs looped over his gun-belt, the town looked normal now. Gone was the fear that had spread through the townspeople like a sudden rush of bone-chilling water sheeting over them when they saw the three killers walking slowly toward the sheriff's office. Everything looked so peaceful now. In fact, were it not for the numerous bullet holes and broken glass in several buildings and storefronts around him, most already covered with plywood, and the three large dark spots on the street in front of him, it would have looked like a typical end to a typical day.

But it hadn't been a typical day.

Those three dark spots marked where three of the "baddest-of-bad men" had died trying to kill him, each man's lifeblood seeping out to stain the dirt in the street. He had stood his ground that day and done what he had to do, even though a pair of holes in his hat and the grazing wound on his right arm still stung and burned, reminding him of just how close he had come to death.

As he was reliving the dramatic fight that filled the street with thunder, lead, and three dead men's bodies, suddenly the sheriff's head jerked to his left. Voices were calling out his name. The tension inside him from rewinding the showdown in his mind instantly melted. An audible sigh, a smile, and then a flood of warmth came over him; for the voices belonged to a tall, strapping boy and a fair-haired young girl.

His daughter got to him first, running ahead of her brother and mother, jumping right up into her father's strong arms. After hugging her close, he set down his daughter as his wife and son walked up to him. He put an arm around his son, looking warmly at the young man who looked so much like he had as a youth. Then the sheriff turned to look at his wife and found her eyes full of tears.

The tears poured from beautiful blue eyes. They spoke not of sadness but of an immense relief as she reached out and hugged her husband, burying her head in his wide shoulder. Sobs of relief, mixed with heart-swelling pride, showed on her face as she pushed herself back and looked up at her husband. And then she kissed him hard, right there on the sidewalk in front of the kids and the townsfolk who had stopped to look at this impromptu family reunion.

She had reason to be proud of him. He alone had faced up to those killers. He alone had done what had to be done to secure their family's future and the future of their town. With a heart full of love and admiration, she said to her husband, . . .

2°

"Sir, sir, you need to wake up, sir."

Sir? Somehow the words didn't seem right.

As he opened his eyes, it was a woman's voice talking to him all right, but it wasn't his wife's voice. As Brian shook his head, he finally began to realize where he was *and who he was.* He'd been dreaming of course. He wasn't a hickory-tough, six-foot-two-inch sheriff, standing surrounded by his loving family after a high noon standoff. He was just *Brian.* A middle-aged, exhausted, out-of-shape, barely five-foot-eight-inch salesman. And he wasn't standing on a wooden sidewalk. He was sitting, squeezed into a window seat in row 32 of a packed, thirty-three-row aircraft.

The woman who had spoken to him was a flight attendant about the same age as his son, and she hadn't gone away like the woman in his dreams.

"Sir," she said, "can I ask you please to put your tray table up and pull your seat forward for me?" she said condescendingly. "Thank you."

Then, as if in afterthought she felt she needed to explain her reason for waking him up, she leaned back and mentioned, "The captain has told us that we're probably going to hit some turbulence coming into Denver, with the rain and all." She turned and moved up the aisle to continue her passenger checks.

Brian nodded his head and began to move to comply with her instructions. That meant picking up the thin paperback western novel and half-eaten bag of chips lying on the small tray table in front of him. After putting up his tray table, he looked down and brushed the crumbs off his more than middle-aged stomach. Finally, after a struggle, he got the seat belt fastened around him, wondering again if it was time to get one of those seat-belt extensions he'd seen a few other people use.

The whole time he did this, Brian ignored the person in the middle seat beside him, as was his custom. As alone as he could be in a row in coach, shared with two other oversized men, he turned to look out the tiny window beside him, trying to see any lights down below.

Just clouds. He thought to himself. *Rain and turbulence.*

Then the thought came to him, *Looks like my life.*

And indeed it did.

chapter three

2°

how low can you go?

As Brian slept, the United Airlines flight he was on had transferred directional control to DIA tower, joining a long line of airplanes making their gradual descent into Denver. As the pilots watched their instruments up front, far in the back of the plane, Brian's dream of being "large and in charge" like that sheriff remained surprisingly vivid in his mind's eye. Unfortunately, as he came more and more awake, he realized that his *real* life couldn't have contrasted any more with his dreams.

Brian's dream had been filled with pictures of courage, strength, and clear convictions. Images still lingered of a warm family relationship and of a man who had an overwhelming sense of a job and life well-done. Now, as he forced himself to stare out the window, Brian felt simply overwhelmed. Instead of a whole town looking up to him, Brian felt incredibly alone and about as valuable as a used-up, twisted-up, discarded dishrag. It wasn't for any lack of effort, he knew; but it seemed like the things most important to him were slipping away, and there was nothing he could do about it.

These feelings weren't just brought on by the exhaustion of being at the end of a long business trip. As a road warrior for his company for the better part of two decades, Brian was used to being away from home. What stabbed at his heart was how much of a failure he felt in so many areas of his life.

There was work of course. Brian thought about the fact that he was now the oldest man still traveling a sales route for his company. Of course,

2°

he had been told repeatedly by his superiors that they needed his experience in the field. In reality, Brian knew his job was "on the bubble" at best. Over the years he'd taken courses on leadership and extra training in managing projects. There'd been a time when he felt sure he was going to be asked to move into the main office. But years had passed and the call never came. With all the efforts he'd put into being a good employee, he was amazed at how insecure he felt. And that terrible feeling was just the tip of what was causing his stomach to tighten.

At a deeper level, what bothered Brian even more was the picture of affection, admiration, and genuine warmth shown by the sheriff's wife in his dream. In fact, as he thought about his marriage, his chin literally dropped several inches. As he continued looking out the window, he could picture his wife, Jennie, and the look she had given him before he'd headed to the airport. It wasn't affection or pride he'd seen etched on her face the morning he left but frustration and even thinly veiled contempt. Once again they had spent the previous night trying and failing to get on the same page when it came to problems they'd been having with their teenage daughter. He remembered his wife's cold reluctance even to kiss him good-bye that morning, turning her head when he tried to kiss her so that he barely pecked her on the check. And with a stab of pain, Brian thought about her failure to answer his "I love you" with like words of her own—even though he'd said it twice, as if perhaps she hadn't heard him the first time.

They had been married twenty-two years, and Brian could count nearly as many times that he had tried to reboot his life and attitude in an attempt to be more of the man he felt she needed or wanted. He knew it wasn't his salary that was causing the problem. It wasn't a lack of things causing the growing gap between them. Rather, it was something more intangible. That "something" the sheriff had in his dreams—that confidence, or clarity of purpose, or courage, or leadership, or whatever that was so real in his mind and yet was as easy to lay hold of as a mirage when it came to his everyday life.

As anxious as Brian was about the widening gap between him and Jennie, it was thoughts of his daughter that pulled his chin even lower. There had been a time when his daughter, Amy, whom he now realized was the fair-haired young girl in his dreams, actually did adore her father. Not now, it seemed. On those rare occasions when Brian did see his teenage daughter, she was either firmly closing the door to her room or sitting silently at the table after being forced to come to a rare family dinner.

Work. Marriage. Being a father. It was like he was going through a mental checklist with a huge black marker and checking "failure" after each selection. And if those three areas so important to him weren't enough, he began to think about who he *should* be, which made him think of his spiritual life. Instead of thoughts of his faith giving him comfort, Brian felt like here too was another box being checked "failure."

Brian hadn't grown up going to church, but he'd made a serious go of living out a life of faith after becoming a Christian in college. That meant regular church attendance, as well as all those conferences and challenges from faith-based books and sermons he'd read and listened to—now stretching on for years.

For example, it began for him with a book he'd read nearly three decades ago, right after coming to faith. This book challenged him to "order his private world." This was the first time he'd felt something ring true about the need for a centered, ordered life. It was after studying this book that, for the first time, he captured on paper a whole list of "must make" changes. Yet as the weeks and months went by with no real change in his home, health, or heart, it was also the first time he experienced that gap between wanting to change and really seeing change take place.

Brian remembered as well how just as his enthusiasm for a life of order began to fade, along came another powerful challenge to change. In this case it came via a national men's conference and movement that convinced him to hope once again. He remembered thinking maybe a life of order wasn't the key to change. Changing his focus to center his life on several promises would do the trick.

Brian became not only a participant but a leader in his church's men's ministry. He spent hours calling and encouraging men to be part of filling up an entire stadium in their city, which actually happened. In fact, Brian had even traveled to the Mall in Washington, DC, where over one *million* men of faith had gathered.

2°

Once again all the rallies and conferences he attended acted like emotional stepping-stones across a rushing stream. Unfortunately, if his foot stayed too long in any one spot, that stone would start to sink. He'd have to leap quickly onto the next conference, the next book, the next campaign, all in an attempt to feel like he was moving forward yet never reaching the longed-for other shore.

Then came a time in Brian's life when in addition to all the rallies and large group meetings and gatherings, Brian discovered small groups. The first small group he was in focused all their time on yet another new book with a challenge to move to a more significant life. Once again it sounded just like what he needed. Those small group studies gave him a chance to go deeper and share more honestly than he ever had before, but here again came that nagging problem. As the months again turned into years of small groups, and *while talk of change had been almost constant, there was a glaring lack of real change taking place in his life.*

Then, just as the small-group stone began to sink, Brian jumped at something else that supported him for yet another season. At the church he attended, the entire congregation was going to spend more than a month encouraging each man and woman to get a clear purpose statement. Getting a clear purpose would help them live out a life of vision, meaning, and fulfillment. Out of everything he'd done, this focus on getting a clear purpose seemed the most helpful. In fact, between the sermons and books and small groups, he actually began to "get the picture" of a life of significance, clarity, and purpose. Brian had even laminated his purpose statement and carried it with him in his day-planner in his briefcase.

Yet after making every service and small-group meeting and reading every chapter and filling out every form—*not one year but also year two when the church repeated the study*—here he was, staring out another airplane window at nothing, feeling empty, insecure, and an incredible failure in what was most important to him.

That huge, terrible gap between all the talk and paper plans he'd made and change that never happened, left him feeling incredibly discouraged. Brian had already decided to skip the newest churchwide push his pastor had just announced. Soon everyone in the congregation would start studying how to have his or her best life now, based on yet another new life-focusing book; but Brian had already decided not to join them.

Campaigns. Conferences. Books. Challenges. Commitments. Countless prayers. For almost three decades, Brian had been there, done that, gotten the T-shirt, and then gone back to get the alumni and volunteer T-shirts. All of these things had helped Brian when he was right in the midst of a packed stadium or sitting in a crowded pew at church on Sunday. But somehow, between walking out of a stadium or sanctuary and reaching his car, it was like something crucial evaporated inside him. All the energy, clarity, emotion, and conviction that seemed so real and motivating when surrounded by others never seemed to translate into real change when he was alone!

As he sat on the airplane, Brian tried in some way to picture the frustration he felt. What came to him was like being constantly told about the joys of flying an airplane by an incredibly persuasive pilot. Whatever book, conference, or inspiring teacher he was listening to at the moment was like a world-class pilot turned ground-school instructor, extolling the joys and how-tos of flying. But as soon as ground school ended and it was time for Brian to solo, it seemed like something always went wrong.

Even with his flight plan carefully laid out and color coded and the engines all revved up, he never really took off. He could create plenty of noise and vibration, but he could never figure out how to release the air brakes and really take off on his own! And after all these years, all the dashed hopes from getting to the edge of the runway and yet never experiencing the reality and freedom of flying himself, Brian had begun to feel like he didn't even *want* to try to fly anymore.

Brian stopped looking out the window and rubbed his eyes. He tried to will himself just to stop thinking so much about so many discouraging things, and of course that instantly brought another area of personal concern to mind.

As Brian turned back toward the window and leaned forward to see if any of Denver's lights could be seen, in the back of his mind he also thought about how physically out of shape he'd become. Not that he'd ever been an incredible athlete, but he'd played sports, and once he'd been in decent shape. He had just begun to think about all the diet books he'd bought and exercise plans he'd started and stopped over the years, when suddenly the plane lurched and . . . *Crack!*

The sharp noise came from Brian's forehead smacking into the Plexiglas window. The plane had found the promised turbulence. He rubbed his forehead, feeling for a knot. The plane began to shudder as if a pair of giant hands had grabbed the plane, shaking it. As they came over the mountains into Denver, the plane dropped and shuddered violently. While the wild ride made several people on board gasp, and more than a few of the people on board with even mild religious convictions begin to pray, it caused Brian to think the worst.

As he gripped his armrest, Brian thought for a moment about what it would be like if the plane *did* go down in the storm. While he didn't really want that to happen, of course, in his heart of hearts, this wasn't the first time he had wondered what it would be like if he just wasn't around anymore. Honestly, would things *really* be any worse for his family? Would they even stop for a moment to miss him at work? Rubbing his head in an attempt to get rid of the pain caused by hitting the window and to dispel such depressing thoughts, the one bright spot in his life suddenly came to mind.

While he knew he couldn't take all the credit, he thought about Andy, the outstanding young man who was his son. Brian was surprised it had taken him so long to think of his son after he'd woken up. Normally, every few waking minutes he'd think about Andy and wonder and worry and pray for him. For while it was nighttime in Denver, it was daybreak in Iraq where his son was serving the first three months of what was scheduled to be a yearlong tour of duty with his Marine Division.

No one else was allowed to call his son, Andrew, Andy. Even his mother called him Andrew, at her son's request. But even though Andrew was four inches taller than his father and had the physique of a weight lifter and wrestler, he still allowed his father to call him Andy, just as he had when he was young.

Up-front the copilot, who was actually flying the plane that night, finally dropped below the clouds; and the airplane quickly stopped shaking so dramatically. Brian could now see the lights of the west side of Denver below him, slightly distorted as they twinkled through the rain. The captain came on and said that with the rain the temperature on the ground this late summer night was down to 40 degrees. The last weather report Brian had seen the day before, it had been 118 degrees at the heavily fortified airport in Baghdad where his son was stationed.

Like a number of young men who had watched the Twin Towers fall, Andrew had felt a growing conviction to serve his country. Brian had himself never served in the armed forces, being too young during Vietnam and too old for Desert Storm. They were all shocked when Andrew announced that he was enlisting in the U.S. Marine Corps right after finishing his second year in junior college. But so many things Andrew did surprised his father. Brian had never been a particularly good student. Andrew excelled in school like his mother, especially in mathematics, where Brian didn't have a clue. As a young man, Andrew loved Boy Scouts and building things. Brian had never been a scout, nor had he any mechanical aptitude. Yet for all their differences in personality, Brian knew Andrew loved him, and the two of them had a deep, obvious bond.

I guess that's one thing I've done right, Brian thought to himself, and his mood lifted slightly. But then a voice inside him told him that in reality it had been his wife's steady hand that had had the most to do in shaping Andrew into the man he'd become. And so even here, thoughts of his son generated pictures of that large marker pen checking "failure" once again.

They were on final approach now. Brian thought and prayed to himself: *Work. Home. My relationship with you, Lord. My health. It's just got to get better.*

And that's when his eyes caught a shining glimmer at his feet.

While Brian knew it couldn't be what he thought it was, it looked like the rain outside had somehow gotten inside the airplane and was soaking his briefcase. He turned on the overhead light, and that's when Brian saw what had actually happened.

Before he fell asleep, Brian had nuzzled his two-sips-short-of-a-full can of soda into the seat pocket in front of him. During the turbulence he hadn't noticed that the open can had tipped over, filling the seat pocket in front of him with sticky, liquid syrup. The soda was now soaking through the cloth pocket and steadily dripping onto his leather briefcase and shoes.

They were too close to landing to get the flight attendant to get him some towels. Brian tried to ignore the disgusted look of the passenger next to him as that man tried to move his own bag and feet away from the dripping mess. While not a word was spoken between the two of them, the look Brian got from the man next to him communicated how stupid it was to put a nearly full open can of soda in the seat pocket.

I am a failure and an idiot, Brian thought, his shoes already beginning to stick to the carpet. And turning off the light above him, looking fixedly out the window, it was the tears moistening his eyes, not the rain outside, that distorted the runway lights as they landed.

chapter four

2°

when things just can't get any worse

Wake up, Brian. The phone's for you."

It was a woman's voice again, rousing him out of his sleep. Only this time the words actually *had* come from Brian's wife. After getting off the plane the night before, his shoes sticking with every step, Brian had walked to the underground shuttle train and then on to baggage claim to retrieve his bag. He'd gotten off an airport shuttle bus and hurried through the rain to where his car was parked in remote parking. That meant he still had to drive from the airport located on the far north side of Denver through the rain to his home, almost equidistant on the south side of town. It was well past 1:00 a.m. when he had finally got into bed.

"Wake up, Brian." His wife, Jennie, said, in the same voice she had used to wake up their children when they'd been late for school. She tossed the phone handset on the bed next to him. "You slept in again and missed your accountability group," emphasizing every syllable of the word *accountability.*

This wasn't the first time Brian had slept in instead of getting up early enough to make his group meeting. For almost two years Brian had been part of a small group of three men who attended the same church. Just a few weeks ago his group had added a fourth member. This new man was actually the newest assistant pastor at their church. His name was Eric, and he was the one on the phone.

Brian tried to push the sleep from his voice as he put the phone to his ear and said, "Hello?"

2°

"Hey, Bro," came the positive voice on the other end of the phone. "We missed you. What's up?"

He's calling me "Bro" because he can't remember my name, Brian thought. He barely knew Eric. The man had been a surprise hire to fill their vacant children's pastor's position. Brian had actually been on the search committee for the church that had first seen Eric's résumé. Two years of junior college, then he had enlisted in the army, finished basic training, and headed right to Desert Storm. It was that part of his résumé that had reminded Brian so much of his son and caused him to look in detail at the rest of his résumé After serving honorably and being discharged, Eric had spent two years finishing his degree at Bible college and then spent two more years in seminary learning to be a children's pastor.

"Are you there?" Eric asked, pulling Brian's thoughts back to the conversation.

"Yeah. Sorry," Brian said, groping for an explanation. "Look, Eric, I should have called one of you guys last night, but my plane got in super late with all the weather delays. You know, typical 'planes, trains, and automobiles' stuff."

"No problem," Eric said. "I just wanted to see if you've got anything going for lunch today. I could catch you up on some of the things we were talking about this morning. Brian, we're going through some really cool stuff. You need to hear about it, Bro."

"Ah, well," Brian stammered again, trying desperately to think of some reason he couldn't do lunch. As he started to come more awake, he began mentally to run through his day. It dawned on him that it was Tuesday, which meant he had his weekly scheduled lunchtime meeting with his supervisor—and the excuse he needed not to meet Eric. While emotionally he would rather sit through a root canal than these weekly "slam Brian" sessions, at least it was an excuse not to have to hear about something "exciting" that would just get his hopes up again. He had once known someone who would get as excited about the next new study as Eric obviously was—*him*. Not anymore.

"Sorry, Eric," Brian said, "but I'm locked up every Tuesday around lunch. I have to meet with my supervisor at work."

"OK. But you get off pretty early in the day, isn't that right? How about coffee around 4:30 p.m. before you head home?" Eric asked.

Brian was now fully awake. There was a voice in the back of his head telling him that if he said no to coffee that afternoon, then Eric would just ask about breakfast, or lunch, or coffee tomorrow, and if not then, the *next* day, and if not, the next. Slumping back into his bed, he heard himself mouth the words,

"Fine. I can do coffee, I guess."

"Great!" Eric boomed. "Is Roasters good with you? That's near your house, right?" This was a new coffee shop that had indeed opened right down the street from Brian's house.

Agreeing on the time, Brian thought as he pushed the "off" button on the receiver, *At least coffee won't take as long as lunch.*

Brian struggled to reach over and place the phone back in its cradle on the nightstand next to the bed. Then he gave a sigh and willed himself to get out of bed. As he walked past the large mirror on the wall, he caught a glimpse of himself in the XXL T-shirt and running shorts he used for pajamas. One look make him think for a moment about exercising. He should do at least a few sit-ups or push-ups. But then came all the rationalizations. After all, he *had* already missed his meeting. And he really did need to get in to work. He could exercise tomorrow maybe. After winning (or losing) the "I need to exercise" battle, he walked to the kitchen, opened the refrigerator, and pulled out several toaster waffles.

When Brian walked into the kitchen, Jennie was finishing their daughter's lunch. While there was no way she could have missed seeing him come into the kitchen, you'd have thought he was invisible for all the reaction he received upon entering the room. As she focused on the peanut butter and jelly sandwich taking shape before her, Brian finally spoke.

"Jennie, can we talk a minute?" Brain asked tentatively.

"That's all I've got," Jennie said, flatly. "One minute."

"OK. Well, how are things going at your job?" Brian said, trying to get on some kind of safe ground for the two of them to talk.

"It's going like it always does," she said with no particular emotion in her voice. "Too few of us doing too many things." Jennie was a paralegal in one of the largest law firms in town that seemed to be growing bigger every day.

2°

"Look," she said with a note of finality in her voice, "I can't sleep in like you can. I'm going to be late if I don't get going, so please make sure that Amy gets this." She put the sandwich in a small brown sack on the counter. With that Jennie turned and headed down the hallway toward their bedroom, leaving Brian standing in the kitchen.

He didn't feel a bit hungry anymore. Still, he stayed in the kitchen and ate two toaster waffles. Then he went back and got a third. Each one he layered with butter and then drenched with syrup. If he had thought about it, eating alone and eating food covered in syrup or sauce was more and more becoming his reaction of choice to feeling emotionally like another door had been slammed in his face.

His stomach now uncomfortable with all the "comfort food" he'd eaten, Brian rinsed his plate, put it in the dishwasher, and then slowly went down the hallway to their bedroom. Jennie was already out of the shower, dressed and leaning forward, looking in the mirror, putting on her eye makeup.

He walked past her without comment and took a shower. Jennie left for work while he was showering without a word of good-bye. He dried off and walked into the walk-in closet. He slowly began to dress, thinking about Jennie and then thinking about the "dressing down" he was sure to get from his boss at their meeting later that morning. Brian also thought about the jumble of emotions he'd felt the night before brought on by his dream.

As he stood in the closet, his mind distracted, it finally dawned on him that he had taken down two pairs of pants in a row from their hangers and tried, and failed, to get them to button around his stomach. One look at the row of pants that were left convinced him that taking down another pair from the closet was futile. He gave up and walked into the bedroom, unzipping his travel bag that he'd left there the night before. He retrieved a pair of pants with an even larger waist that he knew he could wear. He also knew he was now down to two pairs of pants that would fit him, both of which he'd taken on his trip. Time to go up another pants size.

Brian took his daughter to school that morning on his way to work. Trying to start a conversation with her was like trying to start a car with no gas in the tank. After several sputtering attempts, he dropped her off with barely a word having been spoken between the two of them. As he left the student drop-off zone and headed to his office, he looked down on the passenger side and saw the brown paper bag lunch down where Amy's feet had been. Once again she had "accidentally" on purpose forgotten the lunch her mother had made her. If Jennie knew she'd gone off without her lunch . . .

Right then, if someone could have measured Brian's discouragement level using an emotional rain gauge, it would have measured 100-percent full from all the emotional storms he'd weathered just the past few days. What he didn't know was that the gauge was getting ready to overflow.

"Take a seat," came the words from Brian's supervisor, gesturing dismissively at one of the two side-by-side, padded, straight-backed chairs in front of his desk. Like he did every time he saw his boss, Brian couldn't help thinking about the way certain people looked remarkably like their dogs. Actually, he didn't mean it in a cutting or negative way. Brian didn't even know what kind of dog, if any, his supervisor had. But from the first time Brian had seen the man sitting in front of him, the word *boxer* had come to his mind. Indeed, his supervisor had an overly large head covered with brown, bushy hair, a thick neck, large brown eyes, puffy cheeks that hung low, and a mouth perpetually turned down like an upside-down smile. And of course, whenever he sat in front of him, his words always had a bite.

"You didn't close the Weaver account, did you?"

Gone were any pleasantries or questions about how he or his family was doing. Anything resembling a personal conversation had vanished when Brian's previous supervisor, who had liked him, had retired. This new super was all business, always scowling, and hadn't even used his name when he spoke to him.

"We're close," Brian said in answer to his question, meaning every word he said. "It was a good trip. I met with all the right people, and we're absolutely still in the running. I may even hear some good news from them this week." But even as he said these words, he was struck by the negative way the question had been asked. "You didn't close the Weaver account, did you" was a statement, not really a question at all. There was not a shred of optimism in it, like when you walk by someone when they're fishing and say hopefully, "Caught anything?" This was like someone who had a grudge against you walking by and saying, "You fished all night and didn't get a bite, did you?"

There was a long pause before his supervisor answered Brian. There was no expression on his face that he had even heard what Brian said about his trip and the good news that might soon be coming. It was then that Brian saw the single piece of letterhead in front of his supervisor that was now being pushed across the desk toward him.

"This will explain it," he said, with just the slightest hint of a smile showing around his puffy eyes and the edges of his mouth.

"This will explain what?" Brian asked.

"Your probation. It's a step we're required to do with someone who's been here as long as you have." His supervisor said. "I've spelled it all out in writing. Look it over and get back with me if you have questions."

But as his supervisor immediately stood up, it was obvious that if questions were to be asked, this wasn't going to be the time. Brian took the letter and walked back to his office.

Sitting down, Brian thought, *If this is a step in the process, then that means they're finally taking steps to fire me.* As he sat in his chair in his windowless office, he thought of the three days he'd just spent building relationships with key people at Weaver—information his supervisor had dismissed or ignored. Adding probation at work to a fitful night's sleep and his wife and daughter all but ignoring him again, and his emotional rain gauge was definitely overflowing.

Just how in the world am I going to bring up that I'm on probation, or worse, at work? Brian thought as he stared at the letter. He couldn't even talk to Jennie for more than a minute without her clouding up and walking out of the room. Would she sit still to listen to this, or would she walk out of the room or maybe even out of their relationship?

While there had been a time when he'd never have thought such a thing could happen, the icy fear he felt made him think perhaps the unthinkable really could happen. He had never, ever, seen Jennie so angry and distant for so long. It scared him. So too did the list of "performance requirements" he'd just read through in order for him to keep his job.

Brian's heart sank.

Another list, he thought. Another chance at the end for him to check "failure" next to these huge tasks he knew were next to impossible to meet.

Still hurting from the obvious relish his supervisor had gotten in giving him the first step toward dismissal, Brian went about the rest of his day the best he could. He faked enthusiasm as he returned several calls. He read and responded to a flurry of e-mails from the people he'd just met with at Weaver, people who apparently weren't as negative as his supervisor as to their chances at landing their account. Then, just before he headed out the door for his appointment with Eric at the coffee shop and home, an e-mail popped up from his son.

Brian clicked on the e-mail with the memo field marked simply, "Hi, Dad." When the message booted up, he pushed print on his computer. He waited for the short note to print, grabbed it from the desktop printer, and then headed down to his car. If Andy was writing him, then he was still OK. That was good news, no matter what kind of day it had been.

Brian walked to the parking garage, went down two floors, and found his car. He opened the door, got inside, and pulled the door shut. He was going home to show his wife a letter that said he was a failure at work, and the very thought of what it could do to his family made him feel like he'd stepped into an open elevator shaft instead of sitting down in a car. Yet at that lowest of all his recent low points, it was like a ray of sunlight finally pierced the clouds.

Two floors underground, the first of *two* much-needed rays of light came to Brian on that very dark day.

two rays of light on a very dark day

Sitting in his car, Brian realized that he was still holding the unread e-mail from Andy. He wasn't about to have his supervisor come in and find him reading an e-mail from his son on work time, so he had printed and brought the e-mail with him to the car. For all parents with a son or daughter deployed and in harm's way, the Internet has been a tremendous advance over snail mail. Brian and Jennie had even had one live video hookup with Andy since he'd gone overseas, using a line normally reserved for Marine fathers to talk and read stories to their children back home.

Two floors down in the parking garage, there was minimal light, and the inside of the car was dark. So with his index finger, Brian pushed on the dome light above him and then looked down at the now brightly lit words typed and sent by his son a world away.

> *Hi, Dad,*
>
> *We've been a little busy here to say the least. When the TV's on, we get the same cable news you do, so you might have seen some of the pictures they've taken of the 2/II lately.* (While they looked every night, they hadn't.) *If not, that's probably just as well for Mom's sake! I'm still waiting for my big break on TV when they interview me! JK (Just kidding.) We're primarily doing 2 X 2s here.* (Brian knew that meant two days on patrol and then two days off.) *And*

_2_°

most times out we're making some good progress. That's what I wanted to drop you a note about.

Do you remember when I talked to you about our company getting a new lieutenant? He's Marine all the way, but it turns out he just graduated from the Naval Academy, and he's a Christian to boot. Almost every day he circles his three squads together to give us our orders, or he leads a debrief or shares some important news from the theater or back home.

But guess how we close every meeting? Dad, picture this big guy booming out, "One inch!" and we all echo back at the top of our voices, "One inch!" Get it? You see, on some days, it's hard to figure out if we're making progress over here. He drills into us that our job is just to move things forward for the Iraqi people one inch at a time—and that we're one inch closer to going home.

I'm not sure if I'm explaining it right, but it has a lot to do with everything we're doing. "One inch" means we clean and upgrade our equipment just a little bit better every day. "One inch" means we try to win hearts and minds of at least the kids we meet a little at a time by doing small things to help them. "One inch" means we're always moving forward, not giving an inch, but also not putting our focus on the miles worth of work we've still got to do. It's not just slow and steady because when we're out it can be fast and intense. (Brian hated to read those words.) But this "one-inch" thing has really caught on and helped put some things in perspective for me. I guess I get "one inch." Even when I'm tired, I can still do "one inch." And even when things are tough, you can see how we really are making inches turn into feet and yards around here, no matter what they're saying in the media.

I've even decided I'm going to try to do "one inch" when it comes to keeping up with you and Mom as well. There's so much that goes on between the times I can write or e-mail you or Mom, it's hard to sit down and not just freeze up at the computer when there's so much to say. So I've decided I'm going to write you all "one-inch" notes more often. Actually, this note is probably longer than one inch already, so I guess it's working! Love to you and Mom and Amy and *the pup* (Andy's name for their twelve-year-old, slightly arthritic black lab).

> *Dad, just think about that big Marine, pointing with his index finger and saying, "One inch!" when things get tough for you. And remember that God is in control of everything over here and at home. Love you, Dad, Andy.*

One inch. If Andy, who was nearly six feet two inches, said to picture a *big* Marine, the mental image Brian got was of a huge man, barking out those words. He was always amazed at the way his son's words could encourage him. Brian always tried to be positive and encouraging in his letters and e-mails to his son. But Andy's notes, which always ended with his "remember that God's in control" statement at the end of each e-mail, seemed to show up at exactly the right time. He wasn't sure how the "one-inch" thing tied in to the battles he was facing at work and home, but it was tremendous nonetheless to hear from his son via e-mail.

Brian carefully folded the note, backed up the car, and headed to Roasters. Their trademark was, "Better than chain store java." While Brian didn't know it yet, he was about to be handed a coffee *and* another ray of much-needed light and encouragement.

A Cup of Much Needed Encouragement

"Hey, Bro! You made it!" said Eric, when Brian walked into the long, narrow coffee house. With traffic snarled around the popular shopping center, he was late. It was pushing 5:00 p.m. when he walked in. Brian had never been inside Roasters in the late afternoon. In the early morning when he'd been there, the lines were shoulder to shoulder. *This is nice,* he thought. Just a few people were scattered at some of the many small tables, some talking, others using the free wireless they advertised to surf the Web or check e-mail. The man who had called out his name walked up and was now pumping his hand.

"Have you heard from our boy?" asked Eric enthusiastically.

"Yeah, I have," Brian said as they walked over to the counter to put in their drink orders. "I got an e-mail from him just before I left the office. He's still going on patrols and 'staying busy.'"

2°

"Man, we need to keep praying for him," Eric said. "When a Marine says he's 'staying busy' in a hot zone, he needs our prayers."

That wasn't exactly an encouraging thought, but Brian didn't comment about it. They both ordered—Brian an extra chocolate, add whipped cream, hot mocha, and Eric a plain iced Americano. They picked a table next to a window, at the far end of the room.

"OK, Eric, so tell me: What did I miss this morning?" Brian asked, cradling his hot mocha. The smell of his coffee alone made him feel like perhaps this meeting with Eric wasn't such a bad idea after all.

"Remember, you've actually missed *two* meetings." Eric said with a smile. "You were traveling last week, and then there's this week. So I've got a lot to catch you up on."

Brian looked at Eric. He was just slightly under six feet tall, and while he had to be pushing forty, he looked like he could still fit in with a group of twenty-five-year-old weight lifters. His face was unlined, even after all the time he'd spent in the sun in the Kuwait desert. And of course there were those two distinctive features. A "Mr. Clean" style shaved bald head and his rather large, George C. Scott- or John Wayne-type nose. When the search committee that Brian was on had interviewed Eric for the children's pastor position, one of the members wondered in private discussions if Eric's imposing size and "Christian biker" looks would scare small children. In fact, children flocked to him, sensing a good heart under all that muscle. The more he was around Eric, the more Brian appreciated his new accountability buddy as well.

"Well, you need to know that what you missed *isn't* the new study that the whole church is starting," Eric said. "We're going to get to that, but we've decided to take a three-week break first to look at something else, and week one started this morning."

Interested now, Brian took a sip of his mocha while Eric continued.

"During these three weeks we're going to look at something I think you and I really need. I mean, the other guys in our group need it too, but I think you and I really need it in particular."

It wasn't just the hot coffee that made Brian instantly feel slightly hot under the collar. He set down his coffee cup and used a napkin to wipe some whipped cream off his upper lip. Trying, and failing, to keep emotion out of his voice, he said, "So just what is it that *I* need so much?"

After what had happened at work a few hours earlier, Brian was emotionally as sensitive as if he'd gotten an all-day-at-the-lake sunburn. Eric's words may not have meant to hurt, but they stung him like a slap on a sunburned back. For the second time in one day, he felt like he was about to be handed probation papers.

"Don't get so defensive, Bro," Eric said, seeing the way his words had registered with Brian. "I didn't say *you*," corrected Eric, "I said you and me. I think both of us need to look at this, and for a fact I bet I need it more then you do."

After a pause Brian finally exhaled and gave up a little bit of his defensiveness with the breath. "OK, so what is it that you think we *both* need?"

"We're going to look at something called *The 2 Degree Difference*," Eric said. And then he sat back in his chair, smiled, and took his first sip of his Americano.

There was a long pause as Brian expected Eric to continue the conversation.

He didn't.

When it became obvious that Eric wasn't going to say anything until he spoke, Brian finally broke the long silence by saying, "*The 2 Degree Difference?*"

"That's right," said Eric. He reached into the backpack he had brought and pulled out a copy of a book called *HeartShift* and put it in front of him.

"We're not going to go through the whole book right now. We may do that later as a group if we want to. But for a few weeks we're going to talk about the core concept behind this book. Then we'll start the study the rest of the church is doing."

There was another long, uncomfortable pause. Reluctantly, Brian finally gave in and restarted the conversation by saying, "And I'm guessing you're going to tell me just *why* our group thinks this is so important to study?"

"Actually, it was my idea," said Eric. "OK, it was really my wife's idea. You see, Megan was in this study group before we moved here. They went through this *2 Degree Difference* concept. Bro, I'm telling you, I've seen some amazing things happen in her life over the past year."

Brian had meet Eric's wife at the final interview for the children's pastor. Other than that, he'd only seen her at church and said hello when they'd passed in a hallway.

"For example," Eric said, "did you know that Megan's lost almost forty pounds in the past year?"

"So it's a diet book?" Brian said hopefully, thinking about how he had never gone through a diet book in any of his men's groups. That might actually be something he was interested in.

"No, it's not a diet book per se. It's a *thinking* book," said Eric. "It's a book that talks about a concept that gets you to think about your diet and about lots of other areas in your life—but in a different way."

Back to being in the dark now as to just what this 2 Degree concept was, Brian reached for his mocha. From liquid lava hot when he'd first been handed his drink, it had now cooled down to pleasantly scalding. He took another safe sip of his hot coffee. If *The 2 Degree Difference* wasn't a diet book, that actually helped the slight pang of guilt he had felt in ordering a drink so full of sugar that he had joked in the past it was really a "candy bar in a cup."

"Look, Brian," said Eric, "let me put it this way. Are there some areas in your life that you just don't feel are changing or that aren't going the way you want them to go?"

Brian said nothing in response to the question.

"Well, there are in mine," Eric continued. "And before we just reload with another campaign, I think we need to talk about change and especially about this *2 Degree Difference* idea."

Brian hadn't said anything, but his eyes were fixed on Eric, and he was listening closely.

"Look, Brian," Eric continued, "I've heard what you've shared at our small group when you've been able to make it. It doesn't take a missile scientist to figure out that you and Jennie are going through a tough time right now."

Is it really so obvious that Jennie and I are in trouble? Brian thought. He knew he had hinted in his small group that things were challenging at home, but he had only used the usual nonspecific Christian stuff like, "Will you pray for Jennie and me? Nothing big. Just one of those times." Comments like that were all Brian had mustered up the courage to lay before the other men in his group, even if it was supposed to be an "accountability" group. Eric was talking like he'd had a video camera mounted in Brian's house and could see how bad things really were.

"A little over a year ago," Eric said, plunging ahead, "Megan and I were as close to on-the-rocks in our marriage as we've ever been in our sixteen years. I was working in a pathetic fill-in job during the day, on top of working every night when I didn't have classes, trying to finish seminary. I was spending next to no time with the kids, and it seemed the only thing Megan and I talked about was crises, and everything was a crisis." He was gesturing with both hands.

"Bro, I'm talking it was bad. Really bad. I had a job that I hated and was going nowhere. I had no real job prospects until I could get my degree. I was feeling like a failure at school because I just didn't have time to study as much as I wanted and, most of all, like a failure with my wife and kids."

In spite of himself, Brian felt like Eric's words were a mirror reflecting his own thoughts and feelings.

"I'd like to say things started changing because I'm such a great spiritual leader or something," Eric said, "but to be truthful, it was really Megan and the *2 Degree Difference* that made such a huge difference in our marriage.

"I'm telling you," Eric said, bending forward, "it's such a small thing, you're going to think it's not worth talking about this for three weeks. But it's amazing how it got Megan and me started on the same page. It's not that everything changed overnight. But before you know it, things *had* changed for the better." "But before you know it . . . one inch at a time . . . things had changed for the better.

One inch at a time, Brian thought.

Brian wasn't sitting under a vent at the coffee shop, and he still held his hot coffee, but nonetheless, a cold chill made the hair on the back of his neck stand up. In the space of thirty minutes, since reading Andy's e-mail and driving to the coffee shop, Brian was hearing another man he respected share with him about "inches" and how they could make a big difference in someone's life.

"Look," Eric said, leaning forward again, and this time lowering his voice even though there was no one at a table within earshot, "maybe I'm reading things all wrong between you and Jennie. If that's the case, then I'm sorry. But I've got to tell you, at the last few group meetings you attended, you sounded a lot like I did when I was struggling so much with Megan."

Brian's silence was answer enough.

"What's more," Eric said, "This 2 Degree thing isn't just something to do with a marriage. I mean it really helped me get through work and finish a couple of really big projects at school. It even helped me with my kids."

Picking back up his Americano, he said, "So what do you think? Are you ready to hear about the *2 Degree Difference?*"

What Brian was thinking was that he was experiencing a fear he'd only known a few times before in his life. It wasn't a fear linked to any words he thought Eric might share with him. Rather, it was a fear that came when something amazing happened that he just couldn't pass off as luck or coincidence. Brian couldn't shake the fact that both Andy and Eric had used the same words in talking about change. If it had been a day apart, maybe it would be a "coincidence." But the e-mail from his son in Iraq was burning a hole in his pocket. Brian knew that somehow today and eternity had collided at this coffeehouse table.

What's more, it seemed to Brian that a line had been drawn in the sand in front of him by some invisible hand. While he hadn't told Eric or anyone else in his group, he had already decided he was going to quit the accountability group before this next big campaign the church was starting. He was going to blame his need to quit on all the travel, but it was more than that. It was his feeling that being in a group wasn't helping him either.

Now he felt like he'd been ambushed in this unplanned meeting with Eric and the e-mail from Andy. *Maybe "caught" instead of ambushed,* Brian thought. And in spite of himself, he felt a faint stirring of hope that had been missing for a long time. *What if there really was something to a life of* "*inches*" *and* "*degrees*"? He thought, *What if this really was some kind of* "*divine appointment*" *as it seemed?*

God works in amazing ways, Brian thought again. And he finally nodded his head for Eric to continue. And so it began.

Eric sharing about the *2 Degree Difference* and about how small things could change everything.

could there really be something to a life of inches and degrees?

The coffee shop was nearly deserted now. Every so often the small bell attached to the top of the front door would jingle as a stray person, or occasionally a couple, walked inside. They placed their order at the counter and then headed out to face the drive home; or now caffeine fortified, they'd head off for an evening of shopping. That left the two men at the far table almost by themselves, deep in conversation.

"We talked about four things this morning." Eric said. "They all tie together, but you're going to have to stay with me for a little bit to see just how they tie together.

"So if I confuse you," he continued, "feel free to stop me or ask questions. I'm no Dr. Wheeler, you know. I'm just the children's pastor." Eric said this last statement with a broad grin, referring to the senior pastor at the two men's church who was a noted Bible teacher and seminary professor.

"I'm sure you'll do great," Brian said. "Fire away."

Eric began by first reaching down into his backpack and fishing out a small notebook. Out came several sheets of paper and a pen.

"One more thing," Eric said. "I'm no artist, but I can't talk without drawing or using my hands." He then proceeded to divide the single sheet of paper into four equal-sized boxes. In the middle of the top left box, Eric drew a rectangular shape.

"That's a *window,* in case you're wondering," Eric said, finishing his drawing. While he didn't say anything to his friend, it did help Brian to have the explanation of the poorly drawn window. Then, underneath his drawing, Eric wrote the words, "Positive change starts with fixing broken windows."

Eric reached into his backpack again and out came a book with a smiling face on the cover. He put the book down on the table. "Obviously, this is a book by Giuliani," Eric said, pointing to the smiling picture on the cover of a book with a simple title, *Leadership*. Rudy Giuliani had become famous as the mayor of New York. Then he had gained worldwide acclaim in his handling of the tragedy and aftermath of 9/11. To most Americans, including Brian, his face was instantly recognizable.

"The first thing I shared with the guys this morning was out of his book," Eric continued. "But, before I explain what I mean by this drawing and what I wrote underneath it, doesn't your job take you to New York City sometimes?"

"It does," Brian said, nodding his head.

"I go there about twice a year and have for years."

"So you were there before Giuliani was mayor?" Eric asked.

"Absolutely. I've been going since probably 1983 or so." After a moment's pause, Brian said, "I've seen a lot of changes if that's what you mean."

"That's exactly what I mean." Eric said. "For example, since you were there in the late eighties and early nineties, you probably know that New York City was setting murder records almost every year during that time before Giuliani was elected. There were 1,905 murders in New York in 1989," Eric said, having opened the mayor's book and read a series of statistics.

"In 1990 they crossed over two thousand murders in a single year for the first time with 2,245 homicides. That meant that New York City was the most dangerous large city in the world," he said, with emphasis on those last words. "But then something amazing started to happen, which I guess you probably already know since you've been going there for so long. New York City actually started to become safer. In 1993, the year *before* Giuliani started as mayor of New York, the murder rate was almost two thousand, 1,946. His first year as mayor, 1994, it went down to 1,561.

2°

"Now watch this," Eric said, writing a series of numbers, one under the other, in the box with the "window" drawing. The numbers he wrote were 2,245, 1,946, 1,561, 991, 642.

"By 1996, there were 991 murders. That was the first time the murder rate had been under a thousand in decades," Eric said.

"And during his last year as mayor, 2001, there were 642 murders in all of New York City. I mean, even one murder is too many. But think about it," he said, pointing with his pen at one number after another from the top to the bottom of the list. "That's a 67-percent reduction in the murder rate in the eight years he was mayor."

While Brian wasn't sure where all this was going, and while he thankfully had never seen a homicide while he was in New York, he had seen firsthand how dramatically this great city had changed under Giuliani's leadership. Brian remembered how, after his first trip to Times Square in the 1980s, he had vowed never to bring his wife or children there. It was wall-to-wall porn shops, panhandlers, and squeegee men harassing drivers on every corner, graffiti and worse scrawled and tossed everywhere. One of his key suppliers was right in the middle of Manhattan, and he couldn't believe the people who worked there could put up with coming into the city each day to work. In fact, thousands of New Yorkers weren't putting up with it; and individuals—and entire companies—were leaving the city center in droves.

But then things began to change. From being afraid to go out of his hotel room alone during the day, which was how he felt on his first trip to Times Square, Brian saw an incredible turnaround. So much so, in fact, that by 2000 Brian had changed his mind on his "I'll never bring the family to New York City" pledge. His mind went to his family's last and arguably best vacation with the four of them. They had gone at Christmastime to a beautiful, clean Times Square right before the millennium celebrations. So much was different. People would actually make eye contact with you on the street. A man noticed Brian's family was lost as they all huddled around a map, and he offered them directions. Gone from Time Square were the porn shops, replaced by bright stores and Las Vegas-sized neon lights and signs blazing away next to trendy restaurants.

2°

They had even gone to *The Lion King* on Broadway and felt safe walking back to the hotel with their children when the show ended, close to midnight.

"So what do you think made such a turnaround in New York City when it came to the crime rate?" Eric said, drawing Brian back to the conversation. "At least what do you think Giuliani credits with making so much difference in such a short period of time in crime and many other areas that needed change?"

Brian had experienced the change but couldn't think of what one thing Giuliani had come up with that he credited with being the key to so many positive changes.

"More police?" Brian guessed.

"Nope," Eric said. "Fixing broken windows."

Of course Eric had written those words down under his drawing, but Brian hadn't jumped on the connection.

"According to Giuliani, positive change started with fixing broken windows." These last words were spoken slowly, and now Eric paused, letting them sink in.

"You can read all about it yourself," Eric said, "but let me read you one quote from Rudy's book that explains what he means by 'broken windows.'" And flipping through the book to a dog-eared page, he found the quote he was looking for.

Eric read the words highlighted in bright yellow: "'Sweat the small stuff' is the essence of the Broken Windows theory that I embraced to fight crime. The theory holds that a seemingly minor matter like broken windows in abandoned buildings leads directly to a more serious deterioration of neighborhoods. Someone who wouldn't normally throw a rock at an intact building is less reluctant to break a second window in a building that already has one broken. And someone emboldened by all the second broken windows may do even worse damage if he senses that no one is around to prevent lawlessness."[1]

"Do you get it?" Eric said.

"Positive change is all about fixing broken windows."

"It's giving attention to the *small* things."

Eric didn't wait for an answer but continued, "This morning we talked as a group about just why fixing something as small as a broken window could be such a big deal in fighting crime. And," he said, "we talked for a little bit about what a 'broken window' might look like or be in a person's life."

He paused, not sharing an example from the morning's discussion but saying instead, "Now I'll share some of the things we came up with as 'broken windows' later if you want me to, but first, let me get through all four things we talked about. OK to keep going?" Eric said, looking up from his drawing.

Brian nodded.

Brian did have some questions, but he wanted to hear Eric out. He'd gotten the first point, or at least he thought he did. The big results Giuliani achieved had something to do with small things.

Eric reached down, replacing the Giuliani book in his backpack. Out came a small picture frame that he set on the table. It was a simple brass frame, smaller than a three-by-five-inch card. Turning his attention now to the paper on the table, in the top right-hand corner of the page, Eric drew another rectangle in the middle of the box.

"This is a picture frame," he said, pointing to the drawing that looked much like the window he'd drawn across the page. Again his explanation helped Brian understand the similar and equally bad drawings.

Seeing Brian's struggle to see "frame" in what he had drawn, Eric's eyes twinkled, and he said, "Come on. Cut me some slack! I'm no art major." As if he knew this moment would come, he said, "That's why I brought this frame with me. The guys this morning gave me such a hard time about my drawings, I figured I'd bring an object lesson with me. I'd have brought a *window* if I could have put it in my back pack!"

They both laughed as Eric then went on to explain his second point.

"Here's the second thing I shared this morning. It has to do with writing a book, a big book like a novel. Now let me ask you a question. What's the longest paper you've ever had to write for school or work? As in, how many pages?"

Brian thought for a moment. "Probably a term paper in college. I don't know, I guess probably twenty pages plus footnotes," he said, scouring his memory. "I don't have to write long reports at work, so that's probably it," he finished his thought more confidently.

"So you'd say writing a three-hundred-page novel would be a big challenge, right?" Eric said.

There was a pause, and finally Brian said, "Is that a rhetorical question, or do you really want me to answer that?" He didn't want to say, "Duh" to the question of whether writing a three-hundred-page novel was a big challenge, which was the answer he felt like giving.

"OK, I'll take it you agree with all of us this morning that writing a novel is a big challenge," Eric said, ignoring Brian's sarcasm.

"Now let's say you're the one writing this three-hundred-page novel, and you get stuck. I mean dead stopped, a real writer's block. If that was you, and your editors were yelling at you to get the book done, what would you do to finish the book?" Eric asked.

There was a pause in which Brian tried not to be frustrated by this line of hypothetical questioning. Finally, trying not to sound too annoyed, he answered, "Well, not being a writer, I don't know. Maybe I'd take a vacation or something to clear my head, like head to Hawaii or up to the lake or something."

"Sure," Eric said, nodding his head. "That might work. The guys this morning all picked things like that. But let me read you how one professional writer coaches people to get moving and finish a huge project they're stuck on—like an overdue book." Reaching again into his backpack, he brought out another book, this one with an unusual title, *Bird by Bird*.

"This book is by a woman named Anne Lamott," Eric said. "She's a professional writer who teaches classes on how to write books all across the country, and by the way, she's an awesome writer. But guess what she teaches people to do to finish a writing project that needs to get done?"

In answer to his own question, Eric wrote some words under the drawing of the frame as he had with the other picture. Finishing, he turned the paper around so that Brian could read the words right side up.

"Big challenges fall to one-inch frames."

"Let me read you what Anne Lamott tells people who get stuck." And Eric flipped to another dog-eared page and began to read another high-lighted quote:

> I go back to trying to breathe, slowly and calmly, and I finally notice the one-inch picture frame that I put on my desk to remind me of short assignments. It reminds me that all I have to do is to write down as much as I can see through a one-inch picture frame. That is all I have to bite off for the time being. All I am going to do right now, for example, is write that one paragraph that sets the story in my hometown, in the late fifties, when the trains were still running. I am going to paint a picture of it, in words, on my word processor. Or all I am going to do is to describe the main character the very first time we meet her, when she first walks out the front door and onto the porch. I am not even going to describe the expression on her face when she first notices the blind dog sitting behind the wheel of her car—just what I can see through the one-inch picture frame, just one paragraph describing this woman, in the town where I grew up, the first time we encounter her.[2]

"Get it?" Eric said, picking up the picture frame and this time handing it to Brian to hold. "When writing a book becomes a challenge, she doesn't just sit down and try to write the whole book at one sitting. She does it by trying to write just enough words to fill in a one-inch picture frame."

While Brian thought that she actually writes about the mental picture she sees inside that one-inch frame, again he didn't argue with Eric. As a salesman, Brian had spent years learning quickly to read what was being shared. There were now two pictures on the page and two concepts that were in many ways saying the same thing.

Giuliani had faced the huge task of turning crime around in New York City and had done it by focusing his and others' efforts on something small, like fixing broken windows.

Now a writing coach, faced with a huge project ahead of her and a deadline unmet—meaning lots of pressure—would write just enough to fill a small frame. Or as Eric had written, "Big challenges fall to one-inch frames."

2°

"Let me give you one more example of what she's getting at with this one-inch frame idea," Eric continued, pointing enthusiastically at the cover of the book.

"Do you know how she came up with the title, *Bird by Bird*?"

"No idea," said Brian, noting to himself that it seemed a very "outside the box" title for a book on how to write a book.

"I'm just going to paraphrase a story she tells in her book. You can read it if you want to. It had to do with something that happened between her older brother and her father. Her father had come in late one night to find her high school-aged brother sitting at the kitchen table. The boy was terribly distraught. Paper and books were scattered everywhere. When his father asked what was going on, his son told him that he was trying to finish a term paper that was due the next day, and naturally he'd waited until that night to begin. Since his dad was a professional writer, the boy asked his father how in the world he could finish what looked like an impossible task.

"Guess what his father said," Eric said.

"No idea," answered Brian with genuine curiosity in his voice.

"I'm not quoting, but his father asked him what his topic was, and the boy said, 'fifty-two birds of North America.' He had waited until the night before to write about fifty-two birds," Eric said, all smiles, as if he could relate.

"His father just stood there for a moment and thought about it. Then he told his son that it was impossible. He couldn't write a term paper about fifty-two birds of North America in one night . . . but he could write it if he wrote it *bird by bird*."

There was a long pause then as Eric let this second story sink in.

In spite of Eric's bad drawings and his constantly fishing in his briefcase, Brian was indeed beginning to see a pattern here.

Take a big challenge in some area of life or work, and what brings change is something small. Fixing broken windows. Writing a paper one inch at a time or "bird by bird," as Lamott said, to finish a book.

In spite of himself, Brian felt himself getting excited. It wasn't a coffee buzz kicking in. Eric hadn't even said a word about anything personal.

He was just talking about reducing crime in New York City and writing a novel, two things Brian knew he would never have to face. But nonetheless, he already felt like there was something here for him, something that just might help.

"How you doing on time?" Eric said, looking around for the first time in a long time, almost like he was coming up for air. "Do you have time for me to keep going?"

"Sure," Brian said to his friend, also quickly looking at his watch. "I'm still doing OK. It's Tuesday, so Jennie's got a meeting until almost 7:00 p.m., and I don't pick my daughter up at soccer practice for a while, so let's keep going. There are two more things you want to share, right?"

"That's right," said Eric, "and this next one is really cool."

Notes

1. Rudolph W. Giuliani with Ken Kurson, *Leadership* (New York: Miramax Books, 2002), 47.

2. Anne Lamott, *Bird by Bird* (New York: Anchor Book/Doubleday, 1994), 17.

a very different case for change piles up

Before I share these next two things with you," Eric said, "I need to run over and grab some bottled water. You want some?"

Brian shook his head and said, "No thanks."

"I've been doing most of the talking," Eric said, by way of explanation. "Excuse me just a second." He walked off to the coffee bar where the young woman behind the counter slid back a glass door to retrieve a bottled water for him.

Brian took the time his friend was gone to look again at the two hand-drawn pictures on the paper in front of him. This certainly wasn't what he had expected to hear or see from Eric. He'd expected a Bible study. Instead, he was hearing about "broken window theory" and "bird by bird."

These two thoughts seemed, in some ways, random and disconnected ideas but then again, not when you really stopped to look at them illustrated on paper or stopped to think about them. To tackle a huge problem, Giuliani had started small, fixing broken windows. To finish a huge, pressure-filled book, Lamott urged starting small, filling in a one-inch frame.

"Here's your water," Eric said, appearing suddenly beside his friend. And as if in answer to an unasked question, he said, "I thought you might be thirsty and just didn't know it." He grinned.

Indeed, Brian was now aware that he was thirsty after drinking his extra-sweet, "candy bar in a cup" coffee. After they had both taken long sips from their bottled waters, Eric continued with the third thing he had shared at their small group that morning.

"Let me draw this for you—and *no* laughing," Eric said, his face attempting to look stern but given away by the smile that still twinkled in his eyes.

What Eric drew in the bottom, right-hand square of the paper was actually the best image of the three, even though it was certainly the most difficult to draw. Brian could actually tell, before he was told this time, that this was someone standing with their arms outstretched, holding up the thumb and index finger of each hand to make a square. Underneath the drawing he wrote the words, "Focusing on small things helps you see unnoticed things."

"This is something I picked up from a friend who's done a fair bit of directing," Eric said. While he didn't specify what he meant by "directing," Brian knew Eric had grown up in California, so his thoughts immediately went to a friend connected in some way with the motion-picture business.

"Have you ever seen a director who's holding up his hands like this to 'frame' a shot before shooting it in a movie?" And of course, as soon as Eric said that, Brian knew he'd been right to think "movies," and he actually could pull up a vivid mental picture of a director, none other than Alfred Hitchcock.

Brian had eaten at a nice restaurant in Hollywood several years before. It seemed that every square inch of wall space in the place was jammed with pictures of movie stars and directors, many of them autographed. Across the table from where Brian sat during dinner that night was a large picture of none other than the famous, Academy Award®-winning director, Alfred Hitchcock. Brian could still remember looking up at the imposing size and intense gaze of Hitchcock, captured in an old black-and-white photograph, his arms outstretched and his hands making that "square" that Eric was talking about.

"Do you know why directors, or even photographers, still make that square with their fingers as they plan out a shot?" Eric asked. Then he added quickly, "Even if you do know, before you answer, let me get you to do something that I had the other guys do this morning.

"I want you to look toward the front door of this place," Eric said.

Brian dutifully looked far across the coffee shop toward the front door.

"Now take your fingers, make that square and look through it," he said, which again, Brian did compliantly.

"Now as you're looking through that square, tell me what you see," Eric said, "just what you see through that square." Brian had thought it would be obvious what he saw through his framed fingers. He'd see the front door, of course. But to his surprise, something else was "framed" instead of the door when he looked through his fingers. Right next to the door was something Brian hadn't noticed, either when he walked in or at any time since he and Eric had sat and talked. His fingers had "framed" a tall, metal rack, filled with birthday and other occasion cards and envelopes standing next to the door.

Brian thought he must have glanced or looked in the direction of that door a dozen times since they'd come in. Yet as many times as he had looked that way, he had never consciously seen this rack of cards. Obviously, he must have seen it. But as someone who rarely pur- chased greeting cards, perhaps his mind had just skipped over it. Now by making his focus *smaller,* the rack seemed suddenly to appear out of nowhere.

"Wow," said Brian involuntarily.

"What'd you see?" Eric asked.

"That rack of cards that I didn't notice before," Brian answered.

"Pretty amazing, isn't it?" Eric said. "That happened to every guy this morning. In fact," Eric said, suddenly becoming more animated, "just picture this scene. It's early this morning, and the place is packed with people getting their coffee for work or just sitting down to read the paper. All of a sudden, here are four grown men sitting together at a little table, all of us facing different directions with our arms out, looking through those 'director's squares.' We got some pretty weird looks alright," Eric said, showing more pride than discomfort from the recollection.

"That's the third thing I shared with the guys. How narrowing or shrinking your focus to a small area often brings to light things you never really saw or noticed before."

So there it was again. A small focus actually brought more to light. Broken windows helped decrease crime. One-inch frames were the key to finishing a novel. Little things make an unexpected or even a dramatic difference in everything.

They were down to the final square to be filled in with one of Eric's drawings. "Here's the last picture, and then I'll share with you something that will tie all four of these pictures together for you."

This time Eric didn't reach into his backpack before beginning. Instead he drew what looked to be a steering wheel in the last open box on the page.

"Let me ask you something, Bro," Eric said. "Now, be honest," he said earnestly. "Would you say that you're a better-than-average driver?"

That brought a smile from Brian. It hadn't been three months since he'd had to go to traffic school *again*. But he didn't hesitate to answer. He felt he was way better than average as a driver. Just because he was a fast driver didn't mean he wasn't better than average. Or at least it didn't in Brian's mind.

"I'm better than average," Brian said. "Humbly speaking, of course," he added.

"Of course," Eric said, "and just to let you know, every guy in our group humbly answered that they were better then average drivers. In fact, in surveys almost everybody in the United States thinks they're better than average!" A fact that brought a smile to both men who wondered who all those worse than average drivers were who seemed to fill the roads.

"This is something I took from the *HeartShift* book," Eric said. "And it's pretty cool if you think about it. Because if you are better than average at driving, guess what you do constantly when you drive?"

Brian was thinking he would answer, "Check the rear and side view mirrors?" when Eric answered for him, "You're a good driver because you constantly make 2 Degree changes with your steering wheel. Think about it. That's what keeps you between the lines," Eric said, mimicking making small changes with an imaginary steering wheel in his hands.

"What keeps you between the white lines is lots and lots of small movements of the steering wheel. In fact, if you're driving down the road and you start making *10 degree changes,* that's when the DUI patrols pull you over!" Eric said, this time making wider turns with his imaginary steering wheel.

"In other words, it's 2 Degree changes that keep you safe on the road, that keep you between the lines. Or, if you want to look at it from the other direction, do you know what happens when people fall asleep at the wheel?"

"Crash?" Brian responded quickly.

"Well, yeah, but before they crash," Eric answered.

"They drop their hands. They quit steering," Brian said.

"Absolutely," Eric answered, nodding his head. *"They take their hands off the wheel. They quit making 2 Degree changes,* and before they know it—particularly if they've kept their foot on the gas—they're in huge trouble and off the road or worse. You've got to keep making 2 Degree changes consistently if you want to stay between the lines."

While this may have been the most obvious of the four things Eric had shared, it still rang true in a powerful way to Brian, especially when Eric wrote the words under the steering wheel, "Quit making 2 Degree changes and you're headed for a wreck."

There was a long, thoughtful pause as both men looked at the piece of paper before them. All four drawings, as poor and homemade as they were, said much the same thing.

To tackle a huge problem like out-of-control crime, start with something *small* like fixing broken windows.

To finish a major project that seems impossibly big to complete, start with something *small* like writing just enough to fill a one-inch frame.

To bring to light things that are often hard to see, start by doing something *small* by narrowing your focus to a small square.

And to "stay between the lines" when you're driving, you need to do something *small* like consistently making 2 Degree changes.

"Just one more thing about this 2 Degree idea, and then I'll share one thing that can pull together all four of these pictures in a really powerful way," Eric said, his words interrupting Brian's thoughts as he cycled through the four drawings on the page in front of him.

"In seminary, I had to take Greek," Eric said. "You know, the language of the New Testament. What you learn when you take Greek is that many words used at that time were actually 'word pictures.' Like, take the word *self-control* in the Bible. *Self-control* literally means 'to pull in the reigns,' like pulling in the reigns on a horse. And the word *anger* literally means 'flaring nostrils,' like a bull that's mad and his nostrils are flaring. So guess what the word picture is for the word *righteousness*?" Eric asked.

Brian had heard lots of sermons in his day, but this question stumped him. "No clue," he said.

"The word *righteousness* means to 'stay between the lines,'" Eric said. "The righteous person stays between the ancient boundary markers. He keeps his life between the lines."

It wasn't much of a jump for Brian to think how true that was in real life. Just quit doing the small things—quit making 2 Degree course corrections—and you could end up in the ditch spiritually, or in a relationship, in no time.

That thought hit way too close to home, but Brian was rescued from having to think more about it when Eric said, "I've got just one more thing to share with you, and then you'll be all caught up. It's something that pulls together all four of these pictures. In fact, it answers a great secret. It answers *why* doing small things can make so much difference in crime or tackling a big task or staying between the lines. You got time to hear this one more thing?" Eric asked.

Brian looked down at his watch, but he already knew he had time to listen to something that would pull all these thoughts and images together. He was "on call" to pick up his daughter from her soccer practice that night, but even with traffic he could sit for another thirty minutes or so and still be at his daughter's school in plenty of time to pick her up.

"I've got time," Brian said.

"Great," said Eric. "So get ready to learn an incredible secret."

a great secret that grabbed brian's life

It was time to pull the four unrelated drawings together.

On the page in front of him, Brian looked down on four sketches: a broken window, a small frame, a "director's square" made with the fingers of two hands, and a steering wheel. Without explanation Eric drew one more thing.

When they first sat down, Eric had divided the paper into four squares by drawing a single vertical line the length of the paper and then a single horizontal line across the center of the paper. Where those lines intersected in the center of the page, Eric now drew something that Brian recognized as well. Covering that "four corners" areas with a rectangle made to look like a dollar bill, or at least it represented some type of denomination, for it had a dollar sign in the center of the bill.

Before explaining why he had connected all four drawings with an image of currency, Eric asked Brian, "You're familiar with C. S. Lewis, right?"

"Absolutely," Brian said.

While Brian didn't read as many thought-provoking books as he thought he should, nonetheless over the years on countless airline flights, he felt sure he'd read every one of Lewis's books. That included his children's books, The Chronicles of Narnia. And with Narnia now on the big screen, Brian couldn't imagine anyone who hadn't heard the name C. S. Lewis.

2°

"He's an awesome thinker and writer," Eric said, as he once again reached down into his backpack, this time triumphantly resurfacing with a paperback book in hand, *Mere Christianity*.

"Here's what I shared with the other guys. In case you've been wondering, it will help give an answer to why all these small things have so much power to change things in such dramatic ways. You're going to have to put on your thinking cap for a minute to see this, but here goes.

"Lewis didn't discuss broken windows or finishing books or steering wheels," Eric said, "but he did write a great deal about 'small things.' And he especially talked about the concentrated energy for change that comes wrapped up in the smallest of acts, good or bad. But before I give you an example of what he said, I need you to think about somebody at work, or in your neighborhood, that you're having a hard time with. And if there's nobody right now that comes to mind, then pick somebody in your past you had a hard time with," Eric said.

"Can you come up with somebody?" he asked pointedly.

Brian froze. *Are you kidding?* he thought. Was this meeting a setup after all? He hadn't said one word to Eric about being put on probation by "the bulldog" just a few hours ago at work.

Could he come up with somebody? What a question. Every feature of "the bulldog" as Brian sat in front of him, starting with his haughty smirk, came instantly to his mind's eye.

"Brian?" Eric asked, awakening him from his thoughts.

"I think *maybe* I can come up with someone," Brian answered, speaking with rather more emotion than he'd planned on using.

"OK, then," Eric said, sitting back a little as he did. "Just to let you know," he said appraisingly, "every one of us came up with somebody just like that." He snapped his fingers. "So now that you've got that person in mind, here's the question I want you to answer before I read you a quote from Lewis: What's something you could do to start *liking* that person?"

Start liking "the bulldog"? Brian thought incredulously. Caught off guard by the question, he thought that unless he could wave a wand and cause his boss to receive a brain transplant, or better yet, a heart transplant, he couldn't think of anything he could do that would make liking that man possible.

"Here's what Lewis had to say about what has the power to change how we feel about someone, even people we dislike very much." And flipping to a dog-eared page in Lewis's book, Eric began to read:

> The worldly man treats certain people kindly because he 'likes' them. The Christian, trying to treat everyone kindly, finds himself liking more and more people as he goes on—including people he could not have imagined himself liking at the beginning.[1]

"Let me read that again," Brian said, slowly going through the words a second time. Brian hadn't said a word about what had happened earlier at work, but the quote from Lewis did little to push back his anger at his boss for being so rude and unappreciative. To be honest, as he thought back on his day, he wasn't feeling very Christian at the moment, nor did he feel any burning motivation to start liking such a challenging person as his boss.

Eric took the opportunity of Brian's silence to share from his own perspective.

"I felt that way in the army a lot," he said, looking up from his book. "It's easy to like people who help you or stand up for you. But it's really tough to like or even keep a semi-positive attitude toward people who seem to try to make your life miserable—people like one of my drill instructors in Recon school that hated me from the first second he saw me for some unknown reason. And then there was one of the officers I had overseas."

There was a long pause as now Eric was momentarily lost in thought. Finally he continued. "Liking difficult people is a challenge. Maybe not as big a challenge as lowering the murder rate in New York City, but it's a big challenge nonetheless. So let's go back to Lewis," Eric said, exhaling and shaking off old memories of dealing with challenging people. "And let's see what he thinks can overcome this big challenge." He picked up Lewis's book and began reading again:

> The Christian, trying to treat every one kindly, finds himself liking more and more people as he goes on—including people he could

not have imagined himself liking at the beginning. The rule then for all of us is perfectly simple. Do not waste time bothering whether you 'love' your neighbor, act as if you do. And soon as we do this we find one of the great secrets.[2]

Eric looked up from his book. "You're listening, right?" he said to Brian, "because this is huge. You're about to learn what Lewis calls one of the 'great secrets'—the power source or 'enzyme' or 'catalyst' or 'active ingredient' or whatever you want to call it behind all of these pictures we've been looking at." Eric pointed to each drawing in turn that he'd drawn on the page.

"Here's the 'great secret' behind why small things can bring so much change," he said. But Eric needn't have asked if Brian was listening. He was fully alert.

Brian let Eric continue his reading:

> The rule then for all of us is perfectly simple. Do not waste time bothering whether you 'love' your neighbor, act as if you do. And soon as we do this we find one of the great secrets. When you are behaving as if you love someone, you will presently come to love him. If you injure someone you dislike, you will find yourself disliking him more. If you do him a good turn, you will find yourself disliking him less. This is because good and evil both increase at compound interest.[3]

Eric spoke these last words very slowly and with great emphasis. And after a short pause to let the words sink in, he continued:

> And that is why the little decisions you and I make every day are of such infinite importance. The smallest good act today is the capture of a strategic point from which, a few months later, you may be able to go on to victories you never dreamed of. An apparently trivial indulgence in lust or anger today is the loss of a ridge or railway line or bridgehead from which the enemy may launch an attack otherwise impossible.[4]

"Get it?" Eric said. "That's why the dollar bill connects all these drawings." He pointed to the drawing of the bill in the center of the page as he wrote beneath it the words, "Small acts of good or evil grow at compound interest."

He continued, "Small acts—the little decisions you and I make—make an investment in our life story that will multiply, whether we realize it or not. You're always hearing from financial advisors about the 'miracle of compound interest.' And it is amazing how investing a small amount today can compound and become a lot over time. But did you ever realize that there is a compounding effect in our actions and decisions? Small investments—small acts like fixing one broken window—don't just *add* up; they compound. Everyone knows that huge events, like 9/11, can bring great change. But how many people realize the incredible power in small things that can create major changes as well?" Eric said this rhetorically, continuing with his thought.

"Start by fixing things as small as broken windows, and amazingly, those good acts begin to compound, gaining so much strength that they actually start to hammer down the murder rate in New York City. Write one inch of text, and pretty soon, in spite of being stuck, your words begin to compound; and you've got your book written, even when you never thought you could finish it.

"And," Eric said, pausing before he finished his thought, "start doing small things, positive things, toward someone you couldn't imagine liking, and incredibly, you'll find yourself actually changing how you feel about him or her. Maybe even liking them again or for the first time."

Eric had switched emotional gears as he talked to Brian about this last picture. This was by far the most intense and serious he'd been since they sat down. With a sense of a lawyer making a final appeal to the jury, Eric said, "So that's the 'great secret' Lewis described that we're going to look at for two more weeks in our small group." Slowly Eric leaned back in his chair. "That's why I drew a window, a one-inch frame, a director's square, and a steering wheel," he said, circling each drawing on his paper with his finger. "It's why small changes—2 Degree changes—made today, can add so much to our lives tomorrow.

"It's why Lewis felt," Eric said emphatically and in summation of all he'd said, *"that little things could change everything."*

"I know that sounds like an exaggeration," Eric said, almost like he was expecting some kind of argument from Brian about being too expansive with Lewis's meaning. "But listen to this one last quote, and then I'm done."

Skipping ahead in the same book, Eric turned to another highlighted page. Then as if struck by inspiration, instead of reading the quote himself, Eric handed the book to Brian. "Do me a favor and read this quote for me out loud, will you, Bro?" he asked.

Brian took the book that had been held out to him, and after a slight pause, he looked down at the fluorescent yellow-highlighted words and began to read:

> Therefore, what really matters are those little marks or twists on the central, inside part of the soul, which are going to turn it, in the long run, into either a heavenly or hellish creature.[5]

Neither man spoke or felt the need to speak for a long time after Brian had finished reading the quote. Eric finally moved, reaching out and taking back his book. He began putting the book, along with the small picture frame still on the table, back in his backpack, signaling that their "makeup session" was over. And as he did so, Eric's mood changed from intense to his normal, gregarious self. He picked up the paper he'd drawn on.

"You can keep this," he said, handing the paper to Brian. "These drawings are going to be worth a lot after I'm dead," he said sarcastically.

Then, his eyes narrowing a bit, he asked Brian, "You're going to be in town next week for our morning meeting, right?"

When Brian nodded yes, Eric shouldered his backpack.

"Brian," Eric said, "one last thing. I know we're a church group, and I didn't use a lot of Scripture or anything today, but wait until next week. Keep in mind that if small things really *are* that powerful in bringing change to our lives, then you'd expect to see that reflected in Scripture as well. Right?" Eric left this question unanswered, but he gave Brian a sly smile, like he had a whole tray full of cookies (or verses) under the counter, just ready to pull out and share at their next meeting.

Eric smiled broadly and stuck out a hand, and the two of them shook hands warmly. "Walk you out?" he said.

Brian just shook his head, "No, thanks, *Bro,*" Brian said with a smile, the first time he ever recalled calling anyone at anytime, "Bro." "I'm going to hang here for a few minutes until I have to go pick up Amy."

Brian had already decided that instead of driving all the way home, then all the way back again to Amy's school, he'd just hang out at the coffee shop until time to pick up his daughter from her soccer practice.

"Eric," Brian said earnestly, "I really appreciate your talking with me. Thanks for being so persistent about getting together." Suddenly he felt a little awkward. "It means a lot . . . what you shared."

Eric just nodded, and then he was gone.

Brian sat back down at the small table, his mind spinning. It was several minutes before he slowly took out the e-mail from his son—the one that had asked him to face the challenges in his life "one inch" at a time, just like Andy was doing in Iraq. He set his son's e-mail next to Eric's drawings. That's when he thought about the probation letter he was also carrying. He took that letter out as well and set it in the middle of the table.

There, on either side of the probation letter, Brian saw much the same message, given to him on the *same* day by two men he highly valued—two men a world apart geographically. Yet from opposite sides of the world, on the same afternoon, it was like they joined forces to double-team Brian with the same thought, the same challenge that now sat on this table in front of him.

Small things can change everything.

A Turning Point at a Coffee Table

In the months and years to come, Brian would often look back on this day. In particular, he'd think back to this watershed moment as one of the highlights of his life. For it was after Eric had left that the real battle had been fought.

Once by himself, it took no time at all for those all too familiar fears to flood over him, as they always did at the end of a conference, a sermon, a workshop, a campaign, or after finishing a "change your life today like I did" book. Like so many times before, Brian sat alone with sky-high hopes generated from a persuasive person—this time Eric—telling him things *could* change, things *would* change. But then came the fears that always found him at that moment—fears that brought with them a type of emotional paralysis. Already gone was the feeling he'd had just minutes before, "I can do this. I really can change things." Instead, suddenly all Brian could see were the challenges before him—a mountain's worth of changes in so many areas.

The soaring confidence he'd had just a few minutes before plummeted back down to earth. In its place came the words, *Be realistic. You've tried so many things before, and they haven't worked. This is the same thing. It's not going to work either.* And as if knowing just where to put in the pin to puncture and deflate the last of his confidence, came the thought, *Small things? Are you kidding? You've got big problems.*

And indeed, that seemed like a massive body blow to all that Andy and Eric had been sharing. Both men were indeed telling him to hit singles when it seemed that only a home run had any chance of salvaging his job or of saving his marriage. He had *big* problems facing him. Every fiber inside him seemed to scream out that what he needed was a big solution.

As defeated as he'd felt at times in the past, Brian dropped his head and looked down, deep in thought. And it was at this lowest of low points that Brian sensed someone had moved in front of him, like someone walking up to the table. Brian looked up and his eyes flew open and his mouth went agape. For standing right in front of him was a *big* Marine looking down on him. A man well over six feet tall, dressed in tan and brown desert cammies, his face chiseled and darkly tanned by the sun. He leaned forward, staring Brian in the eyes and tapping his finger on the small table as he said in a level, confident voice, "Forget home runs. Forget big things. *Just one inch.* That's all you've got to do today. Just make one inch worth of difference . . ."

2° 2° 2° 2°

Brian was Presbyterian, not charismatic. He'd never heard voices or seen visions, nor could he say in honesty that he had ever felt God had actually spoken to him before. That's why in the days and months to come Brian knew intellectually that the vision of that "Big Marine" standing in front of him stepped right off the e-mail from his son. That Marine had to be a picture his mind's eye had created of the lieutenant his son had described. *But he had looked so real.* And while he couldn't explain what happened when he heard that challenge to face life "one inch" at a time, he knew that a choice had been set before him—a choice like a line being drawn in desert sand.

For over two decades Brian had approached change in the same way. If you had a big problem, then look for a big solution that could change everything. But now he knew that there was another choice. Perhaps change wasn't best made by making 180-degree changes that so often had left his efforts and resolve in the ditch. Maybe real change came through 2 Degree changes, small shifts of his heart and actions.

Like fixing broken windows, filling in a one-inch frame, shrinking our focus to a few inches to see more—making 2 Degree steering wheel changes.

Whatever had brought him there, that image of a big Marine standing before him had tipped the scales. And so it was that at that small table, just before Brian gathered his keys and headed off to pick up his daughter, he bowed his head and prayed. In his prayer Brian asked Almighty God for his help in seeing and doing the *small things.* He sat there alone, and not a single person noticed that time and eternity had somehow met in that coffee shop.

Brian crossed that imaginary line in the sand that day. In spite of all his doubts and fears, he would face the very real, very huge challenges before him in a different way. While time would tell if there was real power or validly to Andy's e-mail, Eric's drawings, Lewis's "great secret," and a big Marine's "one-inch" challenge, he would start making small shifts that night.

He would start making small shifts, 2 Degree changes, beginning when he picked up a daughter who couldn't stand him.

Notes

1. C. S. Lewis, *Mere Christianity* (New York: HarperCollins, 1952, renewed 1980, 2001), 131.
2. Ibid.
3. Ibid., 132.
4. Ibid.
5. Ibid, 119.

chapter nine

the 2 Degree Difference
challenges a daughter
whose heart is closed

As challenging as things were at work and in his marriage, when it came to order of magnitude, it was Brian's teenage daughter who represented the greatest degree of difficulty. In part it was because Brian had rarely been around girls growing up. He had three brothers, and even his mother leaned toward logic and practicality in a house full of testosterone. Both Jennie, Brian's wife, and Amy, his daughter, displayed a wide range of emotions and feelings. And for Brian, trying to understand their feelings and emotions was like attempting to learn to speak Ukrainian without a book, type, or language tutor.

It wasn't that he hadn't tried to connect with his daughter. He had often taken her fishing, just the two of them; been a volunteer AWANA leader at their church when she was young; and gone to every dance recital and soccer game he'd been able to attend with his travel. But it seemed that now every time Brian tried to make a connection with his daughter that drew them closer, something would misfire. It had gotten so bad that for more than a year, if Brian even tried to communicate with his daughter on some kind of level deeper than a weather report, she would just roll her eyes or say to him for the hundredth time, "You just wouldn't understand."

So it wasn't surprising to Brian that when he picked up his daughter that night in the school turnaround, the car door opened and Amy sat down without a word or without making eye contact.

Once they were on the road, Brian took a deep breath and was fairly certain of the reaction he'd receive when he asked the question, "So how was practice?"

"Practice was fine," Amy said, leaving the end of her sentence dangling.

"What about the rest of your day?" Brian asked, taking the bait.

"You wouldn't understand," Amy said. "I'll just talk to Mom."

And so the usual silence fell back between them. The kind of uncomfortable silence that made even facing the bulldog at work more bearable in some ways than a thirty-minute car trip with his daughter.

Brian's conversations with Amy had always seemed to be one-sided tennis matches.

Brian would lob over a question, and Amy would either slam down his words immediately, make some kind of dismissive comment like a passing shot, or just walk off the court. Only now she was in the car, and she couldn't just walk to her room.

2 Degree changes, Brian thought.

"Lord, give me a clue on how to do this," Brian prayed silently as he struggled for what to do next.

As they drove on, the thought came to him that Amy had been trying out for a school play. Not that he had actually had a conversation with Amy about the play, but he had heard her talking with his wife about it and could tell she really wanted a part.

"Have you heard anything about the play?" Brian asked hopefully, as he began to inch his way through the traffic toward the entrance ramp to the freeway they would take.

Amy shot him a look that was full of anger and suspicion.

"Did you talk to Mom? I told her not to tell you," Amy said, her voice filling with emotion.

"No, I haven't talked with her. What's wrong?" Brian said.

There was a long pause as Amy debated in her mind whether to say something to her father or just default to, "You wouldn't understand."

"Lots" was her single word reply when she finally answered.

Brian hesitated and then said, "By your tone of voice, Amy, I think maybe you didn't get good news about the play."

"You might say that," she said caustically, and then behind her words came that mix of anger and tears that always confused Brian. He could never understand how someone could feel sad and mad at the same time. Amy was an expert at doing so since crossing into puberty.

Another long pause ensued in which Amy cuffed away tears in silence.

"Do you want to talk about it?" Brian asked, trying to sound soothing.

"*No!*" Amy exploded with the fury she wished she could voice to her drama teacher. "That's the problem, isn't it? I *can't* talk. I can't even *read*," she said, and she melted into an emotional silence again.

Any further attempts on the ride home to talk proved futile, particularly when Amy reached in the backseat and pulled out her iPod. Even with her headphones on, Brian could hear the music pounding, an apparently unsuccessful attempt by Amy to drown out her sorrowful thoughts with noise.

When they finally pulled into the driveway, Amy threw open the door, grabbed her soccer bag and backpack full of schoolbooks, and stormed up the sidewalk into the house. Brian didn't gain anything more about what had actually happened at play tryouts at the dinner table. The three of them sat there with all the emotion of a funeral service. But Brian was able to corner his wife later that evening when Amy was in the shower.

"She didn't get the part," his wife said matter-of-factly. "I guess everyone trying out had to stand up and read a long section from the script, and Amy didn't do very well at that. She had practiced saying some parts from the script, but it was reading out loud that seemed to throw her for a loop for some reason."

Brian went to sleep that night, still not sure if he'd received any kind of answer to his prayer about some kind of 2 Degree change he could make with his daughter. But when he awoke, a new thought came to Brian's mind.

The Morning Memo, he thought, and he quickly went to the computer in Andy's room. It still had his son's posters and many of his things, but it had morphed into the family study and office since their son had left for the U. S. Marines. Quickly going online and pulling up his company

Web site, Brian found what he wanted and printed off a short, two-page document.

Breakfast went as usual, meaning he ate alone at the kitchen table while both Amy and Jennie just grabbed breakfast bars. After dressing and taking his once-a-day-if-he-had-to look in the mirror, Brian and Amy headed to the car for the drive to school.

"Amy," Brian said once they were on their way, "I really need your help on something if you would." After a pause, he continued, "Things are a little tough at work right now, and I need your help."

In spite of telling himself he wouldn't go into any detail with her, Brian found that just hinting at the subject of the probation letter brought more than a flake of genuine emotion to his voice. Perhaps it was that emotion that made Amy take a half step back from her normally defensive posture.

"Like what?" Amy said.

"I need you to help me when we're driving to school by reading me a short sales memo. My boss says I've got to read it before I come in each day. You don't get carsick reading in the car, and it would help me a lot if you could read it to me," Brian said.

"Just read it at night or before we get in the car," Amy said, unhelpfully.

"It's an automated letter that doesn't come in the e-mail until 6:30 a.m. I don't have time before we leave to read it, and it would only take you a minute to help me driving to school. It would really help me, Amy."

Brian had debated whether he should add, "And I'll give you five dollars a week if you'll read to me going in to work." But he didn't like the idea of outright bribery, and so he kept that thought as a last gasp.

His request hung in the air as he continued to drive and Amy pondered the question. This was the small, 2 Degree idea that had come to Brian that morning. He knew that at least part of the reason his daughter didn't get a part in the school play was her struggle with reading out loud. In truth, one of the things on Brian's probation letter was to read his boss's morning memo first thing in the morning. It was a small thing—reading two pages of "breaking news" from his office—but maybe it could help both of them.

Apparently Amy had come to her decision. She huffed, obviously exasperated, and then reluctantly looked down at the printed sheets her father had handed her. With one last great sigh, she started to read the short memo. That day she read to her father about a shipping strike on the east coast and a few other interesting insights linked to their supply chain. It only took her three minutes, tops, and then she was back to her iPod and silence.

That was the beginning: Brian's first attempt at doing a small thing to try to solve a big connection problem between him and his daughter. From that point it became a daily ritual that evolved into Amy getting into the car and buckling up, reaching out without looking for the paper her father handed her, and reading his memo for him. Gradually Brian began substituting short articles he'd wanted to read in place of the workplace memos. And slowly, grudgingly, almost imperceptibly, it seemed that the tension eased a tiny bit between the two of them. And that's when Brian added a second small thing.

As parents of club-level soccer players know all too well, it seems their children in advanced teams are either practicing, playing games, or resting to practice or play games. Brian and Jennie were fortunate that their child's club coach was also a coach at Amy's junior-high school. She had arranged for her club practices to be held at her school field after the team sports were finished. That meant Amy could just stay after school and do homework in the library and then head over to club practice.

With things going fairly well with Amy reading to him in the morning, one evening after practice Amy opened the car door and had to pick up a book that Brian had put on the front seat before she sat down.

Amy just tossed the book by her feet as she got settled in the car, but Brian stopped her.

"Amy, can you pick up that book?" he asked with some trepidation in his voice. "I was thinking that maybe we could read this book together on the way home from practice," he said, trying to sound more hopeful.

"I have to read you a whole book for your work?" Amy said incredulously.

"No," Brian said, "it's not a work book."

Amy looked at the book, *The Lion, the Witch and the Wardrobe,* the first in the Chronicles of Narnia series by C. S. Lewis.

"I know we saw the movie," Brian continued, "but here." He handed her a tiny flashlight from one of the cup holders, twisting its end so that the light came on. Handing the flashlight to Amy, he said, "I was thinking that you and I could read this going home. Or really, you know, that you could read it. But I'd like to hear it too."

"*Dad,*" Amy interrupted emphatically. "It's not like I don't know what you're doing," she said, anger gathering in her voice.

When Brian tried to look surprised, she continued, "You're trying to get me to read out loud. *You know* that's what I did crummy on when it came to getting a part in the play, and you're trying to get me to read out loud." She sounded defiant.

Of course she was right. Reading the morning memos from work seemed to have worked, but this was too obvious, he could see. Brian waited for the rejection that he knew was coming, probably punctuated with more heated words.

Instead there was silence. Just *silence.* Brian had driven out of the parking lot and was looking ahead down the road, not at his daughter. They went through one traffic light. Then another. Then as he eased onto the freeway ramp, Brian heard his daughter's voice: "Chapter 1, The Wrong Door. This is a story that happened long ago. . . ."

Brian almost choked up as he heard his daughter read about a little girl named Lucy who stepped into a magic wardrobe in a game of hide-and-seek. For now there really was a crack in the angry wall between them. Neither of them commented on the small shift that had taken place that night or the subtle way reading just a few pages together had begun to shrink by inches each day the large gap that had grown between them.

That was Brian's first attempt to use the *2 Degree Difference* to change his world, and to his amazement, it had actually begun to work. Next up, an even greater challenge.

chapter ten

the 2 Degree Difference lines up against a marriage that isn't working

One week after Brian met with Eric and decided to start making 2 Degree changes with his daughter, he kept his promise and met with his small group. The morning of their meeting, Jennie was surprised when the alarm went off early and Brian got out of bed first. He headed to the shower and quickly shot off to his accountability group without any grumbling reminder from his wife.

Driving up to the chain restaurant where they always met, Brian and Eric pulled in next to each other, the first to arrive. By the time they had gotten a table, they were joined by three other men, all members of the same church.

Small talk and sports talk flowed freely until a friendly, middle-aged waitress showed up to take their order. She walked away to punch their breakfast requests into the computer that was linked to the kitchen, and as if on cue, Eric called the men to order by taking out his Bible.

"I want to hear what you guys are thinking about this *2 Degree Difference* idea," he said, "but first, let me cover something with you that we didn't get to last week." Eric opened his Bible and turned just a few chapters from the beginning of the book to 2 Kings 5.

"I bet if you guys opened your Bibles to 2 Kings, all the pages would stick together because you've never actually *opened* those pages!" Eric said grinning. A laugh echoed down the table. While it was funny, the looks on each man's face said it was probably true as well.

2°

"I haven't spent a lot of time in 2 Kings either, to be honest," Eric said, "but there's an awesome story here that I think pictures everything we talked about last week."

"I know!" said Darrell, one of the men in the group with Eric's kind of irreverent humor. "It's the story of Elisha healing the broken window!"

After they'd all stopped laughing, Eric said, "Very funny. Actually, Elisha *is* in the story, smart guy. But this is really a soldier's story. It's the story of a guy named Naaman, a great warrior facing a huge problem. So let me try to read it before she brings out our food." Eric began to read: "Now Naaman, captain of the army of the king of Aram, was a great man with his master, and highly respected, because by him the LORD had given victory to Aram. The man was also a valiant warrior." Looking up for a moment, Eric glanced back down and read more slowly, "But he was a leper" (2 Kings 5:1).

"You all know what being a leper meant to Naaman, right?" Eric asked.

Each man nodded, and the mood at the table became slightly more serious now. While none of the men besides Brian had more than a passing knowledge of this particular story, they had all heard sermons, or seen *National Geographic* pictures, or read descriptions in books about leprosy.

Here was a man who had everything going for him, but soon everything would be taken from him. Leprosy was a death sentence in biblical times. Like a pitiless, incurable cancer in our day, leprosy was a slowly creeping loss of nerve function that would begin by claiming fingers and limbs and would finally claim that person's life but not before banishing him or her from all human contact as the disease progressed.

"Naaman was the second most powerful man in his country," Eric continued, "but now he has a *big* problem—as big as it gets back then."

"But here's what happened."

Looking back down, Eric continued reading from Scripture: "Now the Arameans had gone out in bands and had taken captive a little girl from the land of Israel; and she waited on Naaman's wife. She said to her mistress, 'I wish that my master were with the prophet who is in Sumaria! Then he would cure him of his leprosy'" (2 Kings 5:2–3).

Looking up, Eric interjected a question. "Let me ask you guys: Would any of you seek 'alternative medicine' treatments if you or someone you loved had run out of traditional medical options? Has anyone ever *had* to do that?"

Slowly a hand went up at the far end of the table. The man whose hand lifted was named Doug, the oldest man in the group by several years. He was also new to the church and to the men at the table.

"I lost my first wife to cancer," he said. "That was before I moved here and part of why I moved out here." After a pause, he continued, "We found out my wife had cervical cancer. We tried everything when we found out—chemo, surgery. Obviously, we got everybody in our church and all our friends across the country to pray for Bev. But when things kept getting worse, I finally took her to Mexico. We tried several things there that you couldn't try here. It did help her for a little while, but she passed away about a year ago."

"I'm sorry, Doug." Eric said, finally breaking the silence. "Thanks for sharing that, Bro. I didn't know that.

"I guess that's what I was asking," Eric continued. "When you really love someone and you run out of traditional options, all of a sudden lots of people are open to trying alternative medicine. And I think that's what happened with Naaman.

"I think Naaman was probably a pretty pragmatic guy, like most soldiers I know. But when he ran out of traditional medicine options and his wife told him about this prophet in Samaria, I think the idea that someone could not just help him but *cure* him got his hopes up that maybe things *could* change. I'm sure Naaman was a proud guy. He was a leader of leaders, a warrior. But he had a big problem, and so he was willing to listen to this little girl who said there's a big solution in Israel."

Eric was interrupted just then by the waitress coming by with coffee and water refills. "I'll be just a minute on your breakfast," she said cheerfully. They all smiled and nodded appreciatively, and Eric continued after she'd gone.

"Now here's something I love about the Bible," he said. "The people you read about in the Bible are real people. I mean, they react the way real people would react. Take Naaman here. He hears there may be someone who can cure him, but he doesn't just take off. Remember, he's a soldier. He's a commander, no less. So he doesn't just go AWOL. He goes to his commanding officer and asks for leave. And guess what his king tells him?"

Not waiting for an answer to his question, Eric began reading from his Bible again:

> Naaman went in and told his master, saying, "Thus and thus spoke the girl who is from the land of Israel." Then the king of Aram said, "Go now, and I will send a letter to the king of Israel." He departed and took with him ten talents of silver and six thousand shekels of gold and ten changes of clothes. He brought the letter to the king of Israel, saying, "And now as this letter comes to you, behold, I have sent Naaman my servant to you, that you may cure him of his leprosy." When the king of Israel read the letter, he tore his clothes and said, "Am I God, . . . to cure a man of his leprosy? But consider now, and see how he is seeking a quarrel against me." (2 Kings 5:4–7)

"I can picture that." Eric said, paraphrasing the part of the story he'd just read. "Here's the king of Aram, and his best officer is in serious trouble. So when Naaman comes to him to ask for leave to go talk to someone who could heal him, the king doesn't even *consider* sending Naaman to some small potatoes prophet. He sends his captain directly to the top guy. It's like him sending Naaman to the chief of staff at Mayo, not to some alternative medicine guy out in the desert. But the king of Israel can't cure him, and in fact, he tears his robes. Naaman is a soldier standing in front of him, and the king puts two and two together and thinks the king of Aram is trying to pick a war with Israel.

"But then Doug's guess comes into the picture," Eric said, looking down the table with a smile. "Elisha hears about the king of Israel tearing his robes, and he tells the king to send Naaman to him. Let me read you something from *HeartShift* about this that I like." Eric put down his Bible and picked up the copy of *HeartShift* that he'd placed on the seat next to him.

°

"Can you imagine the step down from the king's palace to the bare-bones mud-walled home of a prophet? It would be like leaving the Mayo Clinic, filled with its multi-million-dollar equipment and dozens of renowned physicians and specialists because a rural family doctor had called Mayo to tell Naaman he had misread the address on his appointment card.

"And for the rest of the story," Eric said dramatically as he looked up, "you'll have to wait just a minute." For their waitress, along with a helper, had just shown up with two large trays full of cholesterol and pancakes. Plates were passed down the table and coffee cups refilled. Then Eric asked Brian to give thanks for the food. After they'd said grace and everyone else had started eating their breakfast, Eric continued with the story of Naaman.

"To Naaman's credit, he did humble himself and go from the great palace to the out-of-the-way place where Elisha lived. But when he arrived there, that's where the problems really began." Eric began reading again from his Bible:

> So Naaman came with his horses and his chariots and stood at the doorway of the house of Elisha. Elisha sent a messenger to him, saying, "Go and wash in the Jordan seven times, and your flesh will be restored to you and you will be clean."
> But Naaman was furious and went away and said, "Behold, I thought, 'He will surely come out to me and stand and call on the name of the LORD his God, and wave his hand over the place and cure the leper.' Are not Abanah and Pharpar, the rivers of Damascus, better than all the waters of Israel? Could I not wash in them and be clean?" So he turned away in a rage. (2 Kings 5:9–12)

Eric looked up and said, "I've seen commanding officers in a rage. Particularly if they've got a lot of power, it's pretty serious. And so here's this powerful guy. He's got a huge problem, and he's just been told to go do something by a servant—not even by the prophet himself—and it sounds ridiculously simple. Just to wash in the Jordan a few times and he would become clean. So instead of doing it, he gets ticked off."

Eric asked, "Why do you think he didn't just do what the servant said?"

It was quiet for a moment as the men thought, and some swallowed to clear their throats. Predictably, it was Darrell who spoke first.

"I think it ties in with what you talked about last week," Darrell said. "If Giuliani had actually said to the family of a murder victim or to the press when he started as mayor, 'We're going to reduce the murder rate in New York City by fixing some broken widows,' people would have gotten ticked or at least blown it off as nonsense. It doesn't seem like something that small can make any difference when you've got a problem that big."

Eric nodded in agreement. "That's great insight, Bro. I think you're right. Any other thoughts?"

Brian offered the next thought. "You've said he's a proud guy. Military or not, I think a lot of men and women struggle with pride when they're asked to do something they don't understand fully. I mean, Elisha didn't even come out personally to see Naaman when he stood in his doorway. He just sends a servant out to talk to a head of state. Naaman can't ask any questions. He's just supposed to go take off all his royal robes and go wash in a muddy river. That's asking a take-charge person to take a lot of steps back."

"Absolutely," Eric said. "Great insights. He'd not only have to take off his royal robes, but he'd have to put down his sword as well before he got in the water. He couldn't power his way out of this problem, and that's frustrating if we're a solution-type person.

"So here's the conclusion to this story and to why I wanted to read it to you this morning," Eric said, going back to his reading.

> Then his servants came near and spoke to him and said, "My father, had the prophet told you to do some great thing, would you not have done it? How much more then, when he says to you, 'Wash, and be clean.'" (2 Kings 5:13)

Eric took out a piece of paper that had been folded and put it in his Bible.

"Let me read you that same verse from *The Message*," Eric said. "I love the way it's worded:

> Naaman lost his temper. He turned on his heel saying, "I thought he'd personally come out and meet me, call on the name of GOD,

wave his hand over the diseased spot, and get rid of the disease. The Damascus rivers, Abana and Pharpar, are cleaner by far than any of the rivers in Israel. Why not bathe in them? I'd at least get clean." He stomped off, mad as a hornet.

But his servants caught up with him and said, "Father, if the prophet had asked you to do something hard and heroic, wouldn't you have done it? So why not this simple 'wash and be clean'?" (2 Kings 5:11–13)

Eric emphasized the words "hard and heroic."

"I think that's it for a lot of us. We've got a big problem. We think we need to do something big and hard to solve our problems. Asking Naaman to set aside his pride and go wash in the Jordan seven times, when so much was at stake for him, I think seemed like nonsense. But Naaman did humble himself, and he did do that small thing that his servants said he should. And I think Naaman should be really glad that he had servants with enough guts to face him when he was angry and tell him he was wrong. That's not easy to do with a commanding officer. But they cared for him enough to point out that maybe there was another way than just 'big problem—big solution.' Maybe small things could bring great change."

2° 2° 2° 2°

As Brian drove to work after their morning meeting, he thought back to several stories from Scripture that Eric had shared that morning. Eric had also talked about a time when Jesus explained and illustrated what true greatness was to his disciples. It was putting *one* child in their arms. Not *children,* as if the greatest among them was the one who did the most or helped the most kids. Greatness to Jesus was linked directly with holding *one* child, being "faithful in a little."

This whole idea of approaching change and problems—and now even the steps toward greatness being linked to "small things"—gave Brian a great deal to think about as he drove to work that morning and throughout the day as well.

2°

And so it was that as he drove home that evening, Brian decided to launch the *2 Degree Difference* in his marriage. He'd already made one "small" attempt at 2 Degree change in asking his daughter to read out loud to him in the car. Now Brian would see if small things could mean anything to a marriage he knew was in serious trouble.

2° 2° 2° 2°

Armed with thoughts of fixing broken windows, steering wheels, small frames, verses like, "Had the prophet told you to do some great thing, would you not have done it?" (2 Kings 5:13) and the early success he was having with his daughter in the car, Brian decided he'd tackle the gulf between him and Jennie with baby steps. And the first of those was his decision that once a day he would say a sentence prayer for his wife.

Praying for his wife was one of those "big projects" that Brian had actually started to do several times before over the years. He would read something or hear somewhere at a conference that he needed to "pray for his wife." He'd get convicted and out would come his Day Planner, and he'd block out an hour a day to pray for Jennie. One time he decided to get up an hour early every morning and pray for his wife. That had lasted for about three days. Another time he tried an hour at night. But between work, travel, and the need for sleep, all his attempts met with the same lack of success and the same added dose of guilt with the failure.

What drove all of Brian's previous efforts was linking importance with scale. In other words, if it was important, then it must require a big commitment. He'd never even thought about a sentence prayer for his wife. If it was really significant, and of course praying for his wife was a significant thing to do, then doing something small seemed to minimize the importance of both the task and his commitment.

But now Brian decided to set the bar at one foot, so low that he could hop over it instead of having to make the best jump of his life. Yes, praying for his wife was important, but he decided that short sentence prayers actually prayed, were better than an hour blocked out on his Day Timer and never actually done.

To make it even easier, Brian wore a nice running watch, the kind with split timing features and lap counters. It was something he'd bought in one of his failed exercise attempts but had hung onto because it also had an alarm clock feature he used on the road.

Brian set the alarm on his watch for 3:00 p.m. When the alarm went off, Brian would stop right then and pray for his wife for one minute.

With his 2 Degree change idea in mind, that morning he stopped Jennie in one of her passes through the kitchen. Jennie was in her focused mode in making sure she and Amy got off to work and school on time with that "don't bother me" look about her. Even so, Brian stopped her and asked if there was one thing he could pray about for her that day. Her answer was curt.

"The usual," she said.

"Jennie," Brian said, "I know you're in a hurry, but what's one *usual* thing you want me to pray about. Just one, please?"

His wife fixed a skeptical gaze on him, as if trying to figure out where he was going with this information. Finally she said, "You can pray that I get some of the Nelson case files off my desk."

Offering no more details, she started to charge off to finish getting ready for work, and then she turned and said, "And pray for Andy too." And with that, she was off.

"Pray for case files and Andy," Brian said to himself. "Check. That will be my sentence prayer today," he said, heading off to get himself ready for work.

That afternoon at 3:00 p.m. his alarm watch went off while Brian was sitting at his desk.

Brian had no idea why it was going off when it first beeped. But as he reached down to stop its beeping, it suddenly dawned on him.

"Pray for Jennie," he said, the light going on.

And so that day a small thing like setting his watch to remind him to pray for his wife for one minute started Brian actually praying for her.

By narrowing his focus, he found it easier to do what he said he'd do.

In addition to praying for Jennie, Brian started thinking about other 2 Degree changes he could make in their relationship. Brian knew that follow-through had been a point of contention in their relationship. He could remember one of their first arguments that had taken place when Brian had said to Jennie as he walked in the door, "I love you," and Jennie had answered, "Then go fix the fence."

Brian had explained to her, patiently, that when he told her, "I love you," that she should say, "I love you" back. But Jennie had told him, "Go fix the fence" and *then* she would tell him she loved him. No matter how much they talked about this, it was like they were coming at things from opposite directions, and they never connected with each other. That argument was actually a good metaphor for their marriage.

Brian wanted the *words* so he would be motivated to do *actions*.

Jennie wanted *actions*, which motivated her to share *words*.

But the logjam never broke until Brian decided to link this idea of making 2 Degree changes to small things that were important to Jennie.

After much thought, Brian decided that if he really wanted to test this "small thing theory," then he'd just do one chore, or one small thing a day that was on Jennie's "list." Like many working women, Jennie just didn't seem to have enough time on the weekends to finish everything around the house before it was Monday and time for work again. Brian would pick one small thing to do at home to help.

Pick up the clothes and put them in the hamper.

Perhaps the next day, take out the glass cleaner and wipe down a mirror in their or Amy's bathroom.

The next day, maybe check to see if Jennie's car needed gas or the tires checked.

Just one thing a day.

One small thing.

A feather's worth of change.

Instead of a beeping watch being a reminder, Brian went out to the garage, took one of his old shop rags, and cut off a small, one-inch square of material. He then took a permanent marker and drew the number *1* on the small piece of material. Then he put that one-inch piece of rag in his wallet, alongside his bills and his Starbucks card.

At least once a day, and usually many more times than once a day, Brian would reach into his wallet to take out some money or use his Starbucks card. And each time he would see, or sometimes take out and feel, that one-inch cloth—a "memorial marker" that he needed to do just one small thing a day in his marriage.

When he asked Jennie for that "one thing" he could do, he'd get different responses, depending on Jennie's mood. One time it might be, "Just look around and you pick something to do." Or, "You should know without me telling you," if she was frustrated over a bad day at work. But as the weeks passed, you could tell Brian's request to do just one thing when he got home was getting more specific responses from Jennie.

"Go through the house and change all the lightbulbs that are out." Or, "I can't see the top of the workbench in the garage, and I've got to do some things this weekend out there."

Over the weeks Brian kept up his short sentence prayers for Jennie and Andy when his running watch beeped. And he would look for and do just one small thing a day when he was home, and he'd call and ask specifically for one thing to do when he got back from a trip.

That was it. The sum total of his 2 Degree changes in his marriage that he still didn't fully believe could make much difference. But believing what he'd read and heard that small acts could grow at "compound interest," Brian kept doing them. Brian started opening the car door for Jennie when they went somewhere.

The first time he had done this, he had gotten a shocked look that was a mix of, "Do you want me to drive?" and then, "Pleeeassseee." But Brian had stood there anyway with the door open for his wife and then shut it when she got in. If Amy was with them, he'd let his daughter get her own door. Brian didn't try to run around when they got to where they were going and open Jennie's door before she got out. (Actually he tried, but she was always out before he got there.) But time and again Brian opened her door for her, something he hadn't done in a long time.

Would these small changes make any kind of change at all?

2°

the 2 Degree Difference and the incredible shrinking belt

Brian was making 2 Degree changes in his marriage and with his daughter. Soon, another area pounded away at his attention. Things at work were like a literal pounding in his ears.

It started with Brian thinking perhaps he had swimmer's ear, obviously acquired in the shower since it wasn't summer and he hadn't been near a pool. But the pounding and pressure just didn't go away. Finally, the cross between a loud internal heartbeat and a steady drumming caused Brian to make an appointment with their family doctor.

Brian was able to slide in an appointment during his lunch hour and was in and out of Dr. Carrol's office in twenty-five minutes. Brian was amazed it had only taken that long. But he was more amazed at what was causing his ear problem. Because his family doctor had told him that it was his heart, or most likely his heart, that was causing the problem in his ears. That's because just since his last checkup about six months ago, Brian's blood pressure had risen dramatically.

For several years, Brian knew this day had been coming. Dr. Carrol had read him the riot act and told him that he was pathetically out of shape and that he had to lose weight and go on blood pressure medicine immediately. In fact, he was tempted to send Brian directly to a cardiologist to do a stress test and see if there was even a blockage of some sort. The doctor had stopped just short of making the referral, but he did say he wanted to see Brian back in 30 days or immediately if he felt any tingling in his arms or tightness in his chest. He'd been told he was a "walking medical time bomb" and that he'd better take his weight and exercise seriously or else.

Normally this kind of thing would have sent Brian into an emotional gully. Here was yet another area where someone was telling him he had a mountain of changes to make. As he walked out of the doctor's office, Brian thought instead of what Elisha and Jesus had said about small things, about a director's square, and about all he'd learned about 2 Degree changes. And instead of feeling overwhelmed, he felt surprisingly focused.

Well, I've got another big challenge, he thought.

"OK, Brian, let's go get a salad and think through some 2 Degree changes that can get this doctor off my back and this stomach off my front," he said to himself with a smile. And so the *2 Degree Difference* would start weighing in on his weight. Could small changes bring the big changes he needed in his health?

As Brian sat at lunch after his doctor's meeting, he felt he was starting to gain a feel for this idea of making small, 2 Degree shifts. What was starting to "creep him out" now was how often this idea of making small changes showed up all around him. Like a figure/ground drawing, Brian suddenly noticed what must have been there all the time, but he hadn't noticed. It was like you could see applications of this "one-inch" or 2 Degree concept everywhere.

For example, while Brian was driving in the car and listening to the radio, he had heard a public service announcement highlighting the government's latest attempt at getting people to live healthy lives. He dismissed most of the commercial as background chatter, but his mind came fully awake when the announcer gave out the Web site: "Just go to www.smallsteps.com for information on becoming more healthy."

"Small steps!" Brian had said to himself. "It's everywhere."

And indeed, what movie should come on when Brian was on his next trip? He had crawled into the hotel after a tough sales day and flipped on the tube. Without even changing the channel, there was Bill Murray playing a deeply disturbed counselee in a hilarious sketch with Richard Dreyfuss playing a psychologist.

The movie? *What About Bob?* and the unintentional and unorthodox strategy that Dreyfuss employed was to have "Bob" make "baby steps" in order to get better. In many funny ways "Bob" does just that and seems to get better, much to the chagrin of his doctor!

Baby steps! Brian thought.

"That's what we've been talking about for weeks. I'm taking baby steps!" he chuckled to himself as he went to sleep after the movie ended.

Almost every one of Brian's many attempts at exercise or dieting had come either at the heels of New Year's (in the form of a health resolution) or during play-off time for some sport when he sat and watched incredibly fit people running around on the screen. Or it was motivated by those rare occasions when he actually looked at himself in the mirror, which Brian did as infrequently as possible, after someone had "accidentally" said something cruel or insensitive about his stomach.

In short, Brian could count dozens of failed attempts at decreasing his waistline. And just as in his marriage, the more out of shape he got, the more Brian felt that the only thing that was going to help was something big and dramatic. And now the doctor had as much as told him that he had to do something big and dramatic now! He had to start dropping lots of pounds and taking lots of pills if he wanted a chance of not having his chest opened up.

That fear-based motivation would normally have driven Brian to pick another huge health project. Only now what stopped him was his decision to employ the *2 Degree Difference* instead. As Brian sat and thought and ate chicken salad at a fast-food restaurant, he forced himself to think about this new challenge differently. He got out paper and pen to record his ideas.

He would start making 2 Degree changes in his health, exercise, and diet—small shifts like eating one salad a day.

Brian was looking at the salad in front of him and thinking about how it wasn't really that bad, not that he'd had that many salads recently to compare. But eating one salad a day, for lunch or dinner, could be a small step. As "one salad a day" went on the paper in front of him, he thought about apples too. For at least one or two weeks, Brian had been on almost every diet imaginable. When he'd cycled through his Adkins "meat and more meat" phase, he'd gotten out of the habit his mother had built into his days growing up. The old "eat an apple a day to keep the doctor away" line he'd heard her say a million times came back to Brian now.

That's something else, Brian thought. *I could eat one apple a day. That's small.* And then he added one more small thing to his list.

"Walking."

This was hard for Brian to write down. In part it was pride. He simply didn't look at walking as exercise, even though he knew how valuable it actually was to his health. But with friends like Steve from high school who was running miles each day to stay in shape, walking seemed so embarrassingly small.

But all those talks and verses about "small things" tag-teamed Brian in his mind and challenged him to put down his pride and start small.

"Baby steps," Brian said again to himself with a smile.

OK, I'm officially a walker now, but I'm going to go early so no one sees me! he thought. And then he knew that not being a morning person, he simply wouldn't get up if he set a goal of getting up in the dark each morning. *No,* he thought. *I'm not an early in the morning walker. I'm an "after dinner or sometime before bed" walker. That's when I'm going to walk. It'll still be dark so no one will see me, and I've got a better chance of doing it.*

Brian wrote down that he would walk just two times a week, not every day. Brian thought that his "two times a week" decision ought to make Eric's head nod in agreement when he shared with his friend what had happened at the doctor's, and what he'd decided to do about it.

Eric had come to Brian's mind because the two of them had been keeping in regular contact ever since their evening at the coffee shop. Not just at their small-group meetings in the mornings when Brian was in town. Now they talked on the phone almost every other day. Eric asked how things were going, and Brian kept running things past him when it came to his 2 Degree change ideas. It had come to the point where Brian knew if he made it small enough, it would pass Eric's muster, meaning it was a good starting point for change.

So there it was in front of him on the table—three whole things to change his health and get the doctor off his back—and he'd done it himself—a plan that would get him moving toward meeting his doctor's orders and had a real chance of being lived out for more than a day.

Walking. Eating one apple a day. Eating one salad a day. Pretty simple. "Baby steps."

It was a start. And Brian just added these small changes to the small changes he was doing with his wife and daughter.

"Lord, may these small steps indeed grow at *compound interest*," he prayed as he paused for a moment before throwing away what was left of his salad and heading back to work.

The *2 Degree Difference* was being invested in Brian's home and health. Now there was the huge major matter of being on probation at work. Brian knew that was the next thing he had to face and the next thing that had to be faced with small things.

the 2 Degree Difference attacks a stacked deck at work

So far Brian had taken what he'd learned about the *2 Degree Difference* and begun to apply it in his relationships at home and in making major changes in his health. But like "Mount Doom" that loomed above the whole landscape in the *Lord of the Rings*, Brian knew that the greatest challenge still lay ahead of him. What could he do to try to save his job?

At the last small-group meeting where the group had focused on the *2 Degree Difference*, Eric had shared one last example that came to Brian's mind as he thought about work.

"Let me share with you one more thing from Giuliani's book," Eric said. "Remember how he began to put in practice that 'broken window theory' of fighting crime? Well, early on, in addition to the murder rate, Giuliani decided to tackle another huge problem affecting the city back then. Does anyone remember the squeegee men who used to be on every corner of every street in New York City?"

In their small group both Brian and Doug had seen the squeegee men up close and personal. They had driven in downtown New York City when packs of these men would jump out when a light turned red and "wash" an unsuspecting motorist's windows. Then they would demand payment for their "services." If the driver didn't pay up, they'd often flatten his antenna or kick or dent his car or stand in front of his car even after the light changed until they were paid something. For tourists or business people coming into the city, it was a terrible problem and dangerous as well.

Eric continued, "When Giuliani took over in 1993, the best *estimates* from his police chiefs were that there were more than *two thousand* squeegee men in downtown New York City. Using that 'broken window theory' of looking for small ways to make things better, he decided to take on the squeegee men one stoplight at a time. The mayor's legal advisors told him that there was nothing they could do if these men just stood on the sidewalk. But the moment they stepped into the street they were legally trespassing and could be ticketed.

"And if a policeman gave someone a jaywalking ticket and they didn't have proper identification, then the police could take them into custody for questioning. What they soon discovered was that many of these squeegee men had outstanding warrants, so they were arrested at the police station and taken off the streets.

"So guess what began to happen when they started with just that one, small way of fighting crime? Or, actually," Eric said, "instead of guessing, let me read you what Giuliani said happened."

And Eric read another quote from the mayor's book *Leadership*:

> [We] discovered that there were only 180 squeegee men in the whole city. Nobody could believe it—estimates usually said that there were at least a couple of thousand. . . . If someone would have told me, at a time when we were celebrating making so much headway against 180 squeegee men, that we would end up reducing crime by some 5,000 felonies per week, I would have strongly doubted it . . . but that's the power of starting small with success—by combining several small victories, we could achieve the larger result.[1]

"Pretty amazing, right?"

The men all noted agreement or gave silent assent to Giuliani's amazing results.

"But even though that's another great example of doing small things to make big changes, I shared that example with you for another reason," Eric said. "Did you notice the number of squeegee men they originally thought were terrorizing the city? More than two thousand, right? But while it was still a real problem, it ended up there were only 180 squeegee men.

"What I mean is that when we face big challenges, it's easy to exaggerate how bad things are, even to the point that we think we've lost before we even start fighting, or to think that our abilities are so tiny, we absolutely can't do anything to change things."

Eric then went on to share another example from the Bible that linked with his point illustrated in the Giuliani story. This Bible story was much more familiar to the men in the group than the last one because it had to do with the twelve spies that Moses sent out to spy out the promised land. Most of the men had heard or read how a dozen spies, one man from each of the twelve tribes of Israel, had crossed the Jordan and spied out the promised land that God said he had given them. But when the twelve came back, only two—one man named Joshua and the other named Caleb—said they should go ahead and enter the land of promise. Asking them to keep in mind the "squeegee men," Eric read them these verses:

> Then Caleb quieted the people before Moses and said, "We should by all means go up and take possession of it, for we will surely overcome it." But the men who had gone up with him said, "We are not able to go up against the people, for they are too strong for us." So they gave out to the sons of Israel a bad report of the land which they had spied out, saying, "The land through which we have gone, in spying it out, is a land that devours its inhabitants; and all the people whom we saw in it are men of great size. There also we saw the Nephilim . . . [men said to be giants, Eric explained]; and we became like grasshoppers in our own sight, and so we were in their sight." (Numbers 13:30–33)

Eric finished sharing that morning by commenting on those verses: "Only two men out of twelve had the faith and courage to say that the nation of Israel should go up against those on the other side of the river. Ten out of twelve spies took a long look at the challenges and battle in front of them and magnified them until they were even worse than they were.

"There were real challenges all right and real battles ahead to be fought. But the enemies weren't all so big that the spies were grasshopper-size. If you remember, there was a vote of all the people who had come out of Egypt to decide if the ten spies against or the two for should be followed. Remember what happened? Without a single battle being fought, the people decided that they couldn't win. There were just too many challenges, and there was too little they could do about it. And guess what happened to all those people who voted no? Every one of that faithless generation who said no to taking the promised land died in the wilderness over the next forty years. Only two people who had seen God part the Red Sea got to see him part the waters of the Jordan River—Joshua and Caleb, the two spies who saw the challenge but didn't explode the problem or shrink their abilities. They were the two who led the next group of God's people into the promised land."

And looking around at the men in his group, Eric said: "There were only 180 squeegee men to deal with, but it seemed like two thousand. There were only people in front of them, but the ten spies thought their enemies were giants and they were grasshoppers. Have any of you guys given up before you started to change because you're a grasshopper?"

2° 2° 2° 2°

This last thought about big problems making a person feel like a grasshopper was just the push Brian needed to try the *2 Degree Difference* at work. That's because as he left his group and headed toward his office, he knew that in many ways he felt a lot more like those ten spies than Joshua and Caleb. If the truth be known, he felt like an insect sometimes—small and powerless to do anything to change his situation.

As he processed all this, Brian made two decisions by the time he got to work and found a parking place. First, while it was a small thing, he decided that every day, before he got out of his car at work, he'd tell himself, "I'm not a grasshopper." In fact, he even had the great idea of going by a toy store and getting a rubber grasshopper. It took visiting a few stores, but he finally found a small, plastic grasshopper at the Discovery store that he put in a cup holder in his car. This would be a reminder that he would ask God to make him a man of courage and faith like Joshua and Caleb. And it was to remind him that no matter how big the problems, they weren't big enough to make him feel like a grasshopper.

It hit him after his small group meeting that he must immediately quit referring to his boss as "The Bulldog." Brian was almost never verbally cutting to others. Even calling his boss "The Bulldog" was something he'd only done in his mind, never to a colleague or even to Jennie at home.

Even though his boss did have certain Winston Churchill features that suggested the animal name, Brian knew he'd given him the name "Bulldog" for other reasons as well. Like an angry, snapping, bulldog, his boss intimidated Brian. That picture of cowering like a kitten in front of an angry dog was something Brian realized was behind his calling him "The Bulldog." It was a small thing, a small shift of perspective, but it needed to change. The man might have the power to push him out of his job, but he wasn't a bulldog. He was just a man. And Brian wasn't a kitten or a grasshopper. The second 2 Degree change Brian made was much like the first. He would make a small name change that reframed the way he'd been thinking. He'd use "The Bulldog's" real name from that moment on, which, Brian was ashamed to admit to himself, he didn't even know! He knew his *last* name of course. *Crowley.*

That was the name on his office door and on a black nameplate on his desk. But Brian realized that he didn't even know his tormentor's first name, nor had he ever heard anyone else use it.

Well then, Crowley it is instead of Bulldog, Brian thought. And armed with that small step, Brian would soon take several others, including the small step he made in facing the dreaded callbacks that were on his probation letter.

2° 2° 2° 2°

"Thanks. . . . I understand. . . . OK, then. . . . You bet." Those were the typical things Brian would say when he was on the phone, doing the least favorite part of his job. In most every job, there's one thing that, for whatever reason, is as much fun as chewing tinfoil. Making callbacks was tinfoil time for Brian and had been for years.

Callbacks in Brian's business were code for complaint calls. Something was left off an order; it required a callback. Something arrived later than promised; it required a callback. Someone found a competitor's product cheaper and wanted an explanation and a refund; it required a callback.

Eric was a salesperson, not the complaint department. But in this competitive business world, some upper-level supervisor had decided the company could erase several jobs and their overhead by dissolving the complaint department altogether and just giving callbacks to the salesmen when they came back in from being on the road. No matter that it wasn't their department or their sale. No matter that they all had pockets full of contacts and calls to make when they were off the road and in the office. Every time they got back from a trip, there would be a stack of bright yellow callback slips that were now a part of their job description.

Unfortunately, Brian often put off making his callbacks until it was too late in the day or until it was time for him to go out on his next trip; so they stacked up, undone. It had been reported back up to "The Bulldog"—to *Crowley*, Brian corrected himself—that he wasn't making his share of callbacks. Brian didn't bother trying to figure out who had turned him in or told Crowley he wasn't getting his callbacks done. In part, this was because he knew he *hadn't* been giving a good-faith effort at knocking out those dreaded yellow slips.

These hated callback slips, Brian decided, would bear the brunt of his first 2 Degree change attack. In fact, taking a page from Ann Lamott—who had suggested the idea of a "one-inch picture frame" to authors and that Eric had put on the coffee table several weeks ago—Brian actually went out and purchased a one-inch frame of his own. To find a one-inch frame, he had to go for the first time into a craft store. He couldn't believe how much stuff was there and how crowded the large store was, but he found his frame.

Now Brian cut out a small piece of yellow paper, as close to the shade of the callback slips as he could find. He wrote the number "1" on the paper and then slipped it inside the frame so that the number showed through the glass. Now, along with a picture of his family, Brian had a small frame on his desk, right next to his phone—a reminder that the number one thing he needed to do when he sat down at his desk in the morning or anytime throughout the day, was to make *one* callback.

"Just make one call" was the unstated message in the frame, and to Brian's surprise, he soon started doing one or sometimes more than one callback each time he sat down at his desk. He'd make one call when he first got to work and saw the frame, for reaching for his phone meant almost knocking over the frame. If he went down the hall to get a drink of water or came back from a meeting somewhere else in the building, when he sat back down at his desk, he'd make one callback. And to his amazement, in the course of a day, he'd almost always plow through his pile.

While it was just one small change, that tiny success started a ripple effect in other tasks at work. In fact, all these small things he was doing were strengthening follow-through muscles he hadn't been using in the past. Not that the change happened overnight. But Brian found himself looking at that frame more and more as not just one callback but as a way to say to himself, "Just do one more cold call or one more call to a supplier to see if they could speed up a delivery or one more e-mail to read or send out."

Maybe this is the "one-inch" thing that Andy wrote me about, Brian thought after seeing every callback slip he'd been given in his "finished" box. And that night he sent his son a long e-mail, outlining for him everything that had happened.

Brian shared with his son again how much his "one-inch" letter had helped him and how Eric had met him with the 2 Degree message that same day. He told him about the "Big Marine" that had somehow showed up at the coffee shop and about his small-group meetings and what they'd learned about broken windows, steering wheels, and director's chairs. And he told his son how he had started making 2 Degree changes with Andy's sister with their reading out loud in the car that still continued and "one inch" or 2 Degree changes with his wife by finishing just one chore a day and praying for her when his watch went off. And he told him how he had picked the worst aspect of his job to make a HeartShift aided by that one-inch frame on his desk.

While Brian knew that in the life-and-death world Andy inhabited, these were mundane, everyday things, he also knew from Andy's letters that his son loved hearing them. The everyday things of life back home

2°

helped to bridge all the unworldly things that were part of being a world apart.

Time would tell if these small changes and that one-inch frame would really make a difference for Brian at work, or if Crowley would give them time to work before taking another step.

Notes

1. Rudolph W. Giuliani with Ken Kurson, *Leadership* (New York: Miramax Books, 2002), 43.

the 2 Degree Difference and cold-calling on a new career

Two months had now passed since Brian's meeting with Eric at the coffee shop. Already Brian and his daughter had finished book one and were two-thirds of the way through the second of the five books in the Narnia series. While it went unspoken between them, at the pace they were reading, it was obvious they were going to get through all five by spring. And with each page logged during a car trip to or from school, as well as the occasional errand together, they found themselves lost in the Narnia series, even as they found an unexpected way to reconnect.

If things with Amy had improved dramatically in a short time, things between Brian and his wife, Jennie, looked unchanged after two months. She was still keeping her husband at arm's length. But if the truth be known, in spite of herself, in just those two months' time, Jennie's well-practiced defenses were beginning to show definite signs of cracking. Amazingly, it was opening the car door that had proved to be the tipping point in the huge task of restoring their relationship.

To explain how that happened, it helps to understand her side of the story.

Since the first months of their marriage, Jennie had heard nothing but words, words, and more words from Brian. Every promise Brian made to follow through on a task, or pay attention to something important to her, or to support her in some way with the children seemed in reality to carry as much weight as steam. Jennie often thought of the Bible story of two brothers who were asked by their father to go into the fields and help with the harvest. One boy answered immediately that he'd go, but he never really did. The other son said he wouldn't go, but later he went and did what his father asked.

Brian was that first son.

"Sure, I'll do it!" was the kind of thing Brian would say . . . over and over. And like that first son, the task was left undone. Like when Jennie asked him to put back a slat in their wood fence that had fallen down in a rainstorm. They had a small dog, and Jennie didn't want to worry about Muffin getting out through the hole the missing slat left in the fence.

"Sure, I'll do it!" came Brian's reply when she asked him to put back up the slat. But then it would become too dark to finish the chore *that* day, and then something more "important" would always come up the *next* like Brian's having to go on a work trip. Jennie was convinced that if she hadn't just gone out and nailed in the slat herself there would still be a hole in the fence. Unfortunately, over the years there were fully a hundred requests like that that Brian left hanging. And to Jennie, they represented broken promises, not just unfinished chores.

Jennie worked at a law firm as a paralegal. She liked it there. It fit her personality. At her office there was a motto she'd been instructed to follow on her first day at the firm: "Your say/do ratio needs to be 1 to 1." Meaning, if you say you're going to do something, then you need to *do* it. Or to put it another way, don't say you will do something if you can't or won't.

Jennie followed that motto at work each day, or she would have been fired. Brian's say/do ratio at home was pathetic. And while he didn't realize it and she had never voiced it, she had long since emotionally fired Brian from her life.

Something as small as not nailing a slat to the backyard fence, *like he said he would,* or forgetting to fill up her car with gas so she didn't run out, *like he'd promised he would,* or failing to mail the bills for Jennie that she'd asked him to put in the mail that day, *like he assured her he would,* weren't just little omissions. They were big enough to create a huge gap between them.

As months pushed into years, Jennie felt she couldn't count on her husband. And like many women, she found it terribly hard to give herself freely to someone she couldn't trust. At first, cutting herself off from Brian emotionally and physically had been an unspoken way to motivate him to stop his behavior. But Brian's behavior didn't change. It wasn't that Brian was a bad person or husband. He worked hard to provide for them materially, he was faithful to her and a committed Christian, and he tried to be a good parent. But he had no idea that all his investments he was sure he was making were actually being erased each day, in some ways like the ancient story of Ulysses's wife.

Ulysses was a warrior who went to war and was gone for seven years. During that time, no one, including his wife, heard a word from him. After such a long time, it was presumed by all but Ulysses's wife that the great soldier was dead. As such, a number of suitors took up residence in Ulysses's home, demanding that she pick one of them to be her husband. Believing her husband was still alive, Ulysses's wife told these men that when she finished weaving a large tapestry, she would choose one of them to marry. But unbeknownst to them while she would sit in front of them and weave all day long, she would also unravel all she'd done each night.

That's what Brian was doing time and again in their relationship. Any credit he might have gotten from working hard to provide for them or working hard to be a "good person" was consistently undercut by his lack of doing the things Jennie felt she needed to have done. She would stay with him because of Amy and because of her vows and faith. But she had *zero* feelings toward her husband except for contemptuous and angry ones. And all his spiritual talk of change just distanced her even more from him, not less.

This then was Jennie's heart attitude when Brian decided to start making sentence prayers and small changes in order to make things better between them. And perhaps it was because of how long Jennie's heart had been closed toward him that Brian set no expectations that things would change anytime soon.

2°

It was good he had low expectations, for they were certainly met.

For all Brian could tell, the Grand Canyon gap between them hadn't narrowed a single inch in two months. For example, his wife hadn't given him even a shred of positive feedback about any of the 2 Degree changes he made. Normally, not hearing positive words would have drained away Brian's commitment to continue, but not now—not when all he was doing was just one small thing, once a day. If Jennie didn't have a list to give him or *wouldn't* give him a list of things he could do, he'd still look for that one small thing a day to do and do it.

Like most working wives and mothers, Jennie often felt overwhelmed with work, home, and parenting—particularly with a husband who traveled a great deal. Over time she had steeled herself to the fact that she couldn't count on her husband. So when Brian started doing all these small things to help her, her first response was anger! She didn't feel motivated to say, "Thank you," She wanted to spit out to him, "So where have *you* been all these years?" For a time early on, she was even suspicious, like maybe he'd done something he shouldn't have. Perhaps he hoped all this newfound helpfulness would somehow soften the blow when he finally came clean and told her something terrible he'd done.

But no "smoking bullet" conversation took place, and even when she got angry or refused to give him a list, Brian continuing doing small things. And as much as she hated to admit it, those small things *did* help.

Checking the cars for a change. Doing an errand when she asked. Walking the dogs without being asked. Picking up after the dogs in the back, which he'd never done. Picking up something at the store or at the dry cleaners for her without complaint. Not a single one of those was a big thing in itself. But, like taking one small rock at a time out of her daily backpack, remarkably Jennie felt her load at home beginning to lift slightly. But even as she felt her heart start to change ever so slightly, she still wasn't about to let Brian know that.

If you'd asked Jennie to picture her relationship with Brian when he started his 2 Degree shift toward her, she'd have said that the door of her heart was not only slammed shut; it was also rusted and padlocked. But for two months, without encouragement or thanks, he had kept doing small things. And then he added that one additional thing. And whether from the cumulative effect of his actions or for some other unknown reason, that one thing acted like a pry bar, forcing open a crack in her heart.

That crowbar was Brian opening the car door for her.

At first, when Brian walked to her side of the car and opened the car door for her, she thought it was because he wanted her to drive. He hadn't. He was just opening the door for her. Like he used to do about twenty years ago. Her first automatic response was to roll her eyes. She thought that Eric or someone else in Brian's small-group, which he was now attending faithfully, must have given him an over-the-top idea to try out on her. But while she couldn't explain it, that small act of opening the door did impact her. And as he continued to do that small courtesy, it continued to wrench open the door of her heart toward him, even when she wanted to slam it shut again.

Jennie had been determined not to trust or care for Brian again. For years, she had been able to explain away his words, "I'll change!" *But Jennie couldn't explain away Brian's actions.*

Not that those two months had been perfect. She thought back to the night when Brian had shown her the probation letter he'd gotten from work. That had launched a bitter argument, or at least she'd been bitter. She had felt for years that Brian hadn't fought hard enough at work or demanded that his job be changed. Frankly she wasn't surprised they'd used him up and were now going to spit him out, and in many ways she felt he'd let them do that to him.

Jennie had expected Brian to blame the probation on his boss whom he'd always gripped about. But in sharing the letter with her, the excuses didn't come. Instead, for the first time in a long time, Jennie saw a Brian that reminded her of the "old Brian"—the one who actually had confidence that things would be OK, even if they didn't work out at work.

Jennie also watched in silent amazement as Brian began to make personal changes, like changing his diet. Eating one salad a day was new, to say the least. Going for a walk in the evenings was new. The last time he had started an exercise kick, she had to pick him up at the lake on his bicycle with a flat. That had been more than a year ago, and she'd never seen him do anything positive in terms of eating or exercise since.

2°

But now Brian was going for walks in the evening. Not long walks. Just a block or two, maybe three. Usually taking the dogs, who loved this new after-dinner outing. Watching him do little things to make a difference in his health had actually made Jennie want to be more consistent in her exercise and eating. His prodding her to be more consistent with exercise—or anything—was a first!

And then of course there was what was happening between Brian and Amy. Jennie had become used to the tension level between father and daughter being sky-high, causing strain among all of them as a result. But it was like the tension on a bowstring being gently, slowly reduced. Amy's attitude had softened somehow. Amazingly, the change between them had made things easier for her in dealing with her daughter as well.

In spite of herself, Jennie knew she was beginning to feel something for her husband that she hadn't felt in a long time—a grudging respect and right behind it even the smallest bit of affection. She was so lonely after having emotionally moved away from him for so long. She was so lonely but still so afraid this would turn out to be just a fad or it wouldn't last. Yet as those small things kept coming, the day came when even Jennie couldn't deny that they were inching closer together. Like on the day that she reached over and held Brian's hand in church when they had stood to sing a worship chorus—something she hadn't done in what seemed like forever.

It was at this time, when Brian was seeing significant changes with his daughter and even grudging, unspoken credit gained with his wife, that things took a dramatic turn at work.

2° 2° 2° 2°

"Brian, Mr. Crowley wants to see you."

The voice coming through the telephone intercom on Brian's desk was Crowley's new secretary. Brian didn't think much about this telephone page or the need to go see Crowley that day. After all, it had only been two months since he'd got the probation letter, and Brian had just been keeping his head down, working his one-inch frame every day at work. He knew he was doing more in the office and having better results on the road than he'd had in a long time. And while the probation letter hadn't given him a specific time frame, Brian also knew from other people who had been in similar situations that company policy normally involved a review after *six* months.

The travel schedule! Brian thought. *That's it.* And he felt the issue was settled. It was almost the end of the month after all. Brian was always called down to Crowley's office to pick up the next month's travel schedules and distribute them to the sales troops.

Brian walked down the hallway to Mr. Crowley's office. The door was open, and he knocked on the door frame.

"Come on in and sit down," Crowley said, without looking up.

Brian took a seat in front of his boss and waited. Mr. Crowley finally glanced up, and while still finishing writing something on a note pad with his right hand, he picked up and handed Brian a piece of paper with his left.

Brian had to turn the paper over to read it, and as he did, he tried to remember where the worst weather in the country was this time of year. It seemed like he was always being sent to Phoenix in August and Grand Rapids in January.

But this wasn't a list of trips and cities. The words were short and to the point.

He was to meet with the HR director that morning to talk about his severance package and to have her explain to him what retirement benefits he qualified for. There was mention of a "noncompete" letter he'd be required to sign before he could get either his severance pay or retirement benefits.

And at the bottom of the letter were words that made him sit back: "Date of termination: Effective immediately."

Nearly two decades at the same company and no gold watch. Just two words: "Effective immediately."

Brian sat and read the letter through several times. The third time through he knew that none of the words on the page were going to disappear. He also knew that for twenty years he had tried to be a professional. He was hurt, confused, but he wouldn't yell or make a scene. He'd go out a professional.

"OK, then," Brian said finally, standing up. He started to turn away. Then he turned back, walked a few steps, and reached a hand across the desk to shake Crowley's hand.

"Thanks, Mr. Crowley." Brian said. "I'll be going to see the HR director."

There was a pause, and then Crowley, without standing, reached out his hand and shook Brian's hand. Brian turned and started to walk out.

"Brian," the voice came from behind him.

Turning, he saw that Crowley had stood up now.

"It's just sales. It's all numbers. You did a good job since I handed you that probation letter. I put a letter in your file saying you are a hard worker. You can use me as a recommendation if you want."

And then after a pause, "If you would, give all your files to Edwards and brief him on your accounts. He knows you're going to talk to him this morning."

Brian wanted to ask about one hundred other questions, but that was it. Meeting over. But compared to the three years in which Brian had received a thimbleful of praise from this boss, the words, "You did a good job," and, "Use me as a recommendation," were like a bucket of praise being poured on him.

"Thanks, Mr. Crowley," Brian said. "I appreciate that." And he meant it.

Brian walked past the secretary who was stationed outside his now *former* boss's office. Even though he'd only met her a few times, he noticed now that she was trying hard to look preoccupied with something on her desk so as not to have to look up and make eye contact with him.

He would go to HR in a few minutes. Then he'd go track down and see Edwards and turn over all his sales files. But first he wanted to talk to Jennie if he could get her on the phone. As he headed down the hallway toward his office, Brian was surprised at something. Brian didn't have on new shoes. Just the same old road-warrior Rockports that he'd resoled twice and put hundreds of miles on in cities across the country. But his feet felt lighter.

He had just been fired, and he had a *spring* in his step. *Not bad for a middle-aged, unemployed guy,* Brian thought.

And then, despite all the uncertainty ahead, he thought, *I'm going to make it.*

And then, as Brian walked into his office and closed his door, he breathed a prayer that even a short time ago he wouldn't have thought could be true: "Lord, we're going to make it."

And then he called his wife to give her the news.

2° 2° 2° 2°

That day Jennie did something she almost never did. She left work and met Brian with a hug at the door. A long hug. That night, after Brian had picked up Amy from practice, the family went out to a seafood restaurant that was one of their favorites. It wasn't a fancy place, but it had excellent food and clam chowder to die for. Brian would be receiving six months' severance, so there was money for dinner that night. And actually, both he and Jennie were surprised at both the length of the full severance package he'd received and the company's decision to pay their medical benefits for six months as well.

That night when he went to bed, he lay awake and thought that this long-dreaded day had gone better than he could have imagined. But it was the next day that started to worry him. He would take Amy to school. But then what?

And the *what* came to him almost automatically now.

He'd go after a new job by breaking down his job search into 2 Degree tasks.

He'd already started on a résumé. He'd take that with him when he took Amy to school and go sit in the coffee shop where he and Eric had met. That was something small he could do. And that would be tomorrow's task. Then he'd start putting together a list of names to call. Again, thinking in 2 Degree terms, putting together a call list didn't seem so huge an undertaking.

Once he'd made his list, he put that one-inch frame he'd brought home from his office on his desk at home. And then he'd do what he'd started at work. Make the hard calls, the cold calls, one at a time. It would be wrong to say that Brian was peaceful as he lay in bed. He felt anxious when he thought about where he would land and even fearful when he thought, *What if I can't find a place to land?* But he didn't feel panic. Plus, knowing he just had to face things 2 Degrees at a time, small steps, took a tremendous amount of weight off his shoulders.

Brian e-mailed his son in Iraq about losing his job and about how things were getting better at home. He got a reply back from Andy that night.

"Only have time for a note. One inch, Dad. You can do it. I love you, Andy"

One inch, broken windows, steering wheels, a warrior named Naaman with a *big* problem who was told to do something small. Thoughts of sitting down with Eric and all he'd learned since then about the *2 Degree Difference* flooded through his mind.

Just finish my résumé tomorrow, Brian finally thought to himself. *A cup of coffee with nonfat milk and finish my résumé.* "That's all I've got to do," Brian said aloud, and with that he fell asleep.

fast-forward: a life of purpose at last lived out

Brian pulled into the driveway of his home, and he and Amy got out of the car. It was after lunchtime now, and the two of them had left the house before dawn that day. Brian had just successfully, if slowly, finished his very first "duathlon." Amy had agreed to go as his race crew. While the word *duathlon* sounds impressive, Brian knew he was just taking baby steps compared to many of those who had competed that day. Brian had entered the "sprint" duathlon, meaning he would make a short run of two miles, then ride his bike for ten miles, and then run one more mile.

A year ago, finishing any kind of duathlon would have sounded impossible to Brian. A year ago he wasn't even walking. But slowly, very slowly, he had started to walk. Then jog a little. Then walk. Then walk and jog a little farther. And then his first 5K walk and jog. And then a 10K, now jog and walk. And now, amazingly, he had combined a relatively short run and bike ride. He was a duathlonite.

The race now over, they were home, and Amy got out of the car and ran into the house. Calling out to her mother she said, "Mom! Andrew! Dad won a medal! Come here! You've got to see this!"

And Jennie, who had been in the laundry room, came into the family room where they stood. There indeed was Brian, a red, white, and blue ribbon around his neck and hanging at the end of the ribbon, a shiny round medal.

"Incredible," said Jennie, and she meant that.

Just then Andy walked into the family room from the kitchen, home safely at last.

"Look at what your dad won, Andrew," Jennie said with obvious pride. "You're not the only one in the family now with a medal."

"Awesome, Dad!" said Andy. "I've got to be honest. I was a little worried. The lake race isn't exactly the easiest race you could have chosen with all the hills."

With that Brian looked at Amy and knew he had to confess something.

"Come on, Amy," Brian said. "Fess up. Tell them how I got the medal."

Amy rolled her eyes as if to say that they could have pulled it off if he had just kept quiet. Then she said, "Well, Dad *did* win medal, and he *did* finish the race. But he got the medal because he was the only one in his age class who actually signed up!"

Brian chipped in, "There was nobody *close* to my age. I would have come in dead last in the duathlon, but I sneaked past one person at the end who had blown a hamstring," and they all laughed.

"Are you proud of me, honey?" he said to Jennie, hopefully.

"I think you're crazy!" she said, shaking her head. And then she walked over and held his medal and she gave him a hug. "And yes, I'm proud of you."

Brian's legs were still sore and cramping as the family dispersed, and he went in search of some pain reliever and then a soothing shower. The warm water pulled some of the soreness from his body. He then turned the water on his legs as cold as he could stand it. Brian had read in a running magazine that this might help after a challenging race. The fact that he actually *read* running magazines now amazed him.

Brian dried off and dressed. He sat with a cup of coffee and thought about the past year. So much had happened in such a short amount of time.

Andy's tour of duty in Iraq had ended and with that his enlistment obligations. Without a doubt they were incredibly proud of his service and grateful to have him back home and re-enrolled in junior college.

Amy was getting ready to read for this year's fall play and seemed confident she'd get a part. (The drama teacher as much as told her so in her class.) She was still playing soccer and still reading in the car to her dad. On the way home from practice, they were on the Lord of the Rings books—their latest conquest—having long since finished the Narnia series. And in the morning, on the way to school, Amy was reading some work-related journal articles that Brian needed to hear for his new job.

Brian had landed a job after his *twenty-second* attempt. Eric had told him that twenty-two should be his new lucky number. But Brian had never given up, just kept doing small things to stay on track on discouraging days, and now he actually had a sales manager job with a group that had been a competing company. (They had called Brian right after his non-compete agreement ended.) It was a little longer drive to pick up Amy, but he was loving not having to drive to the airport and get on a plane except on rare occasions.

And then there was Jennie. Jennie had just given Brian a special present for his birthday that past week. She had arranged a weekend away for just the two of them. Dinner at a nice restaurant. Walking arm in arm through streets of small stores in the afternoon, and Rockies tickets for the evening. And the next morning she had given him one more thing. A long, thin box was his present.

When Brian saw the box, his first thought was, *Please don't let this be "man" jewelry.* There was no way he could wear a gold chain and not have Eric roast him mercilessly.

Brian tentatively lifted the cover of the box and was relieved not to find jewelry, but what he found instead was something he didn't get at first. It was a silver-plated ruler for his desk.

But Jennie's note made clear what she hoped it would mean to him as he looked at it on his desk. It was a note that Brian carefully folded up to save, putting it carefully in his sock drawer at home where he knew it would be safe.

It was a short note, in his wife's handwriting. "Thank you for making all those 'one-inch' changes. I love you and am proud of you, Jennie."

All the conferences he'd been to, all the books he'd read, all the campaigns he'd taken part in, all the efforts to change. Brian picked up the ruler from the box and thought it was the perfect gift. The ruler showed so much of what had happened. The small things measured out. All those one-inch steps. "Being faithful in a little." Brian had opted for the *2 Degree Difference* instead of all those huge plans and leaps, and he'd finally found a way to live out that life of purpose and positive change he'd wanted so much.

2°

Journal

Part II

the 2 Degree Difference
journal

*Capturing Your Thoughts and Plans
for Growth and Change*

Important Introduction to the Journal

The story of Brian that you've just read isn't a dream version of what could happen somewhere, someday. It represents the kind of rock-solid life changes that we hear about each week at The Center for StrongFamilies in face-to-face training and in the many letters and e-mails we receive.

In short, Brian's story can be your story as well.

In many areas not even hinted at in Brian's story, the *2 Degree Difference* has made an incredible difference in families, companies, friendships, churches, and individual lives. This journal is your chance to do what Brian, Eric, and their small group did in learning about and applying this powerful concept. Whether you choose to work through this journal with others or by yourself, you'll find probing questions and help-ful activities that will challenge you to lay out a *2 Degree Difference* plan

2°

for those areas in your life where you'd like to make positive change. But before you begin working through the journal, here are several important things to keep in mind.

Outline of the 2 Degree Difference Journal

The *2 Degree Difference* you've just read is meant to be read through just like you would a story, without the interruptions of questions at the end of chapters or sidebar thoughts to slow down your reading. The *2 Degree Difference Journal* will encourage you to do both, to take your time and to work through a series of questions and exercises that we've used with groups and individuals here at The Center for StrongFamilies. In the pages that follow, you'll find:

Part I of this journal will follow each chapter in the book. Sometimes the questions will be focused on the obvious points of the story. Other times, we'll highlight something that may have seemed like a minor note in that part of the story but is worth singling out and listening to on its own. Some will be short sections. Others are much longer. This section can also be used by both individuals and as a discussion guide for small groups or with your spouse or a close friend.

Part II of the journal is your chance to write out your own 2 Degree goals, plans, and actions about that one thing or one area you'll be challenged prayerfully to focus on to see positive change.

Part III of the journal is where you'll find several notes pages for you to capture challenges and successes in living out your 2 Degree changes, additional insights from the *HeartShift* book if you choose to read it, as well as your writing down ways you see the *2 Degree Difference* surfacing in areas or ways you've never noticed before. (Like Brian listening to the radio and hearing about www.SmallSteps.gov, you'll be *amazed* how often "small steps" and the idea of making 2 Degree changes are echoed in Web sites, books, newspaper articles, science or health articles, even business books and workplace programs that promote change.) Now that your eyes are open to the way small things can change everything, this is a place where you can capture different examples of how this concept is applied in the world around you.

For example, let's say you walk into a local bookstore. In the exercise section you might see Jeff Galloways' book, *Marathon: You Can Do It!* If you flip through the pages, you'll discover that this former Olympic marathoner urges both brand-new and experienced runners to run just a short distance—five or six minutes—then walk for one minute. Then you run for five or six minutes, then you walk for one minute, and follow this pattern for the whole marathon! (That's exactly how I ran my first marathon in a blazing 5:21:56 at the 2001 San Diego Rock 'n' Roll marathon.) Now walk over to the business section of the bookstore and pick up *Broken Windows, Broken Business: How the Smallest Remedies Reap the Biggest Rewards* by Michael Levine. Yes, it's based on the broken window theory that Giuliani used to fight crime. Levine tells people in business to focus on small steps for success.

From being successful in exercise to success in the workplace and everywhere in between, you'll be shocked at how many times you're encouraged to make small steps in many different areas. Make note of these examples when they come up here in your journal. Seeing how small steps can bring change in many ways and in many different people's lives can reinforce your own commitment to doing small things as well.

Four Things to Keep in Mind as You Begin the 2 Degree Journal

1. Take your time working through the journal pages that follow.

Here's an important "small-step mind-set." We recommend reading just one section of this journal a day or work through the journal one section at a time with your small group. Instead of simply plowing through all these journal pages like you're trying to get your money's worth out of a college speed reading course, take your time! I realize it's extremely difficult to ask busy people, and especially people who are serious about making needed changes, to slow down. But that's what I'd highly recommend for you to do to get the most out of the journal questions and activities that follow.

2. Remember that small steps are a solidly biblical way of making changes.

If you read Brian's story, you couldn't miss the message that *overreaching* doesn't help us reach our goals or dreams. Taking small steps is a truth you see constantly in Scripture. Part of why Jesus tells us that his "yoke is easy and his burden is light" is because it's true! He's already done the heavy lifting when it comes to setting the stage for us to change our lives. We don't have to pick up huge boulders to become the people we need to be. We just need to do small things like having the faith of a tiny mustard seed.

Jesus offered amazing freedom to those in his day who were weighed down by religious leaders telling them they had to do more, be more, change this, stop doing that. For example, some historians have counted over eleven hundred rules the Pharisees of Jesus' day demanded their followers obey each day!

Jesus sets us free from thinking that more always equals more or that change only comes to the few who can reach the top of the mountain. Instead Jesus looks to reward those who have been "faithful in a little," people who have taken small steps.

Jesus came from the smallest tribe of Israel, was born in a tiny insignificant city, and never owned great wealth or land. Yet it didn't hinder Jesus from doing his Father's will and transforming the world around him. If you remember from Brian's story, Eric shared a story from Scripture about a time when the disciples were arguing about which of them was the greatest. Do you remember what Jesus told them? He said the greatest among them would be the greatest servant, and servants do the small things that help others look and do and live better. Jesus reinforced this with a picture: "And putting a child in His arms He blessed him, and then Jesus said to them, 'Whoever receives *one* child in My name'" (Mark 9:37). In other words, greatness isn't about who launches the biggest children's program, raises the most money to help children, sets up the most children's foundations, does the most for the most children. Greatness boils down to putting *one* child in your arms. Jesus made sure his disciples got the picture that day. The same thing is true in our day. In faithfully doing small things, you and I will find the key to pleasing God, reflecting true greatness, and making the changes we've longed to make.

3. Here are some suggestions if you're going through the journal with a class, your spouse, a good friend, or a small group.

You can certainly go through this journal on your own, and many people do. However, even if you complete the journal on your own, I can't encourage you enough to share what you're learning about the *2 Degree Difference* with a small group, family members, or a trusted friend. If you're married, this book and journal are great tools for encouraging the two of you to talk and make small, positive steps toward even greater closeness. If you're single, look for a rock-solid, "Eric" type friend to meet with you for coffee. Share your thoughts and answers to the questions in this journal. Like "iron sharpening iron" you'll find it helps you gain tremendous cutting-edge clarity and confidence that you can indeed reach your goals.

As mentioned above, the *2 Degree Difference* story is meant to be read through first. Therefore, I'd highly encourage you to make sure everyone in your group has read Brian's story before you work through the journal questions.

Part I of the journal follows the *2 Degree Difference* story, chapter by chapter laid out for a semester study. There are fourteen chapters in the book, so after an introductory meeting to introduce everyone and make sure they've all read their book, you've got a whole semester's worth of questions, activities, and exercises to follow and discuss.

If you're looking for shorter study, at The Center for StrongFamilies we also use these questions in a "two chapters a week" format, making it a seven-week study. We also selectively use questions from this journal in a weekend retreat setting. (Yes, we use the same questions and activities you'll find in this journal, so there's no need to purchase additional small-group materials for your class or retreat. Just follow the questions you'll find here in the way you think best.)

If you're the leader, keep in mind that when people in your group are facing big problems—and many of us are or have in the near past—asking them to make small 2 Degree changes can absolutely go against the grain. Encouraging those in your small group to take small steps can seem like you're urging them to send a mouse out to do battle with a roaring lion. Remember Naaman's angry, prideful reaction to being asked to do something small, like bathe in the Jordan? It was a group of his committed servants and friends who patiently but honestly talked him into doing something small that changed his life.

Additionally, as we do here at The Center, make sure each person in your small group knows this isn't a quick-fix program. It's a process. Brian's story took place over several months. While things turned around relatively quickly with his daughter (to his surprise), it took months and more months before he saw any evidence of outward change in his marriage. If you remember, it was more than a year before Brian had built up enough stamina once he started walking to struggle through a short-distance duathalon (finishing just ahead of the lady with the jogging stroller). Brian also faced twenty-one rejections in his job search before he was able to land a new job on the twenty-second try, even though he finally got a good job that ended up well worth the effort and wait. In other words, it's the process of making small investments and seeing them grow at compound interest that can result in real change.

Another thing we encourage is to make sure those in your group don't set their expectations on never having a single setback day as they seek to live out their 2 Degree changes. Remember, Brian made great strides at his job after receiving that probation letter, but it wasn't enough to keep him from losing his job. There were days when it was cold or dark outside that he didn't get up and walk around the block. There were days he ate poorly before his "one-salad-a-day" goal took root. However, even with setback days, Brian kept meeting with his friend Eric and his small group, and what he learned about making 2 Degree changes helped him stay focused and committed until he *visibly* saw changes take place. That's the powerful thing about doing small things. Most people give up on New Year's resolutions because they don't see success quickly enough. By encouraging those in your group to make small steps, reaching those little goals is self-reinforcing until visible, tangible changes become obvious.

Finally, if you feel you need additional help in building a successful small group—particularly if you're new to leading small groups—then I recommend *Leading from Your Strengths for Small Groups* (Broadman & Holman, 2004). It's a book I coauthored with my good friends and partners at Insights International, Rodney Cox and Eric Tooker. It's a book that looks at a Mount Everest climbing team and then links those insights with a process toward intimacy that can help your small group reach great heights. In short, you can see your small group move up toward intimacy, and you don't even have to wear oxygen!

4. *For those who want to go deeper still, here are some additional suggestions.*

If you're the type of person who in addition to *The 2 Degree Difference* book and journal wants to go even deeper, or if you need "more cookies under the shelf" because you're the one leading a small group or class, then I urge you to order and read the *HeartShift* book (*HeartShift* by John Trent, Broadman & Holman, 2004). In Brian's story and in these journal pages that follow, we simply can't go into the kind of detail that is captured in the 240-plus pages of *HeartShift*. If you haven't already noticed, there is a promotional ad in the back of this book for *HeartShift* along with information on how to order this book from the publisher at www. BHPublishingGroup.com.

Finally, for lay leaders or pastors who want to go beyond personal reading to a certificate training program on the *2 Degree Difference* and other key relationship concepts and tools, I encourage you to go online and learn more about The Center for StrongFamilies. At The Center, we offer outstanding certificate programs for lay leaders, counselors, business team builders, personal coaches, and others who want to coach individuals and teams to make 2 Degree changes in their most important relationships. If you'd like more information on attending one of our certificate training sessions in beautiful Scottsdale, Arizona, or to find out how you can become equipped and certified to launch a StrongFamily center in your home, church, or workplace, look for more information at www.the centerforstrongfamilies.com or at www.strongfamilies.com. Keep in mind that whether you take advantage of any additional reading or training, Brian's story and the journal pages that follow can give you all you need to move forward in courage and confidence.

In the days to come, filled with so many huge challenges from so many directions, it's my prayer that you'll indeed find an incredible peace that comes from doing small things. Through each new season of life, may you live out a life of purpose and promise—one small step at a time.

John Trent, Ph.D., President
The Center for StrongFamilies
and StrongFamilies.com
4718 E. Cactus Rd, #208
Phoenix, AZ 85032
E-mail: StrongFamilies@aol.com

If something in this book or journal proves helpful to you, we'd love to hear from you about the how, why, and what changed in your life. In addition, at The Center for StrongFamilies, we put a huge value on learning, revising, asking for feedback, and actively looking for new ways to help people grow and become all God meant for them to become. In other words, while we've found the questions in this journal to be helpful in working with others, we're always changing and updating pages and exercises. Please feel free to put your own fingerprints all over this journal. Add or subtract as you feel led. If you come up with your own creative exercise for your group that's not in the book and it hits a home run, or if you create a series of questions that you think are even more helpful than those in the chapters that follow, then by all means please feel free to write or e-mail us with your creation! We'd love to hear what you did to make your journal experience even better for you or your group. With your permission your exercise may even end up in a future updated version of the *2 Degree Difference Journal* or on our Web site to help others as well!

the starting place for too many purposeful people

The *2 Degree Difference* begins with the statement, "Because you're reading these words, I know you're busy, committed, and frustrated." How well do you feel that statement actually represents where you are right now? Which part (busy, committed, frustrated) doesn't?

_____

_____

_____

_____

_____

In this chapter, the frustration many purpose-oriented people feel is pictured this way: *"They've prayed and planned; they've read books and gone to seminars; they've attended every focus group at work and small-group meeting at their church, faithfully filled out every handout they were given, and still they feel like their life is stuck at the starting line."* As you think about what you've done in the past to make changes, which of these items in the quote above would be on your list? What else would you add to this laundry list of negatives above that you've tried but failed to find the kind of results you've hoped for?

_____

2°

_____

_____

_____

_____

You may have found more challenges than successes when it comes to taking positive steps forward. Proverbs 13:12 says, "Hope deferred makes the heart sick." On the scale below, give yourself a mark right now on how *hopeful or heartsick* you are that you'll actually be able to make the kind of positive life changes you want to make?

1	2	3	4	5	6	7

Very heartsick and
skeptical that things
can or will change

Very hopeful
that you'll be able
to make changes

Share *why* you chose the number you did?

_____

_____

_____

_____

What number would you have picked one year ago today? If the number you picked is different, what has gone on in your life story that has caused it to go up or down so significantly?

_____

_____

_____

_____

_____

Staying with your choice above on whether you're feeling heartsick or hopeful, let's take an important step back before we take small steps forward. Let's say the Lord allowed us to rewind the clock for a short time so that you were once again ten years old. (Yes, even if you're eighty years old reading or discussing this today, put on your thinking cap and go back to age ten!) Think about the following questions for a few moments:

Where were you living when you were ten years old? _____

What family members were in your home? _____

Where were you going to school? _____

Who was your best friend when you were ten? _____

What was Christmas like when you were ten? _____

If you're in a journal group, have each person go around and answer these questions before you go on. Now choose again a number on the scale below that would have marked your life then as either "heartsick" or "hopeful" when you were age ten:

When you were ten years old, what number would you have chosen?

1	2	3	4	5	6	7
Very heartsick and skeptical that things can or will change					Very hopeful that you'll be able to make changes	

Here's why looking back at who you were when you were ten years old is so important. For most people it is at or right around ten years old when a young man or woman makes up his or her mind to be a pessimist or an optimist. Such an important way of looking at life is often based on what this person has already learned and experienced about change in their early years. Ask yourself (using the questions above and taking time to talk with a family member who was there if needed) what feelings and thoughts surrounded that crucial year of your life.

Were there a great many positive things going on in your world that gave you the message, "I'm moving forward. I can influence the future positively by my actions today." Or was age ten a time when it looked like things would never get better, or at least you didn't feel you had any ability to change things in your world in a positive way? Jot down your responses in the space below as to why you picked the number you did.

_____

_____

_____

_____

_____

For very interesting reading on the impact of "where you were when you were ten years old and why that's so important to understand" check out *Boomers, Xers, and Other Strangers: Understanding the Generational Differences That Divide Us* by Rick and Kathy Hicks.

Here's one last quote and a thought to reflect on from the first chapter.

In a short time you'll read the story of Brian who woke up one day and—despite all the planning, all the praying, all the workplace seminars and weekend conferences, all the church services and heartfelt commitments that things would be different—his life didn't seem to move one inch in a truly purposeful direction. The life he always wanted, his best life now, bore no resemblance to the life he really lived.

Brian's story started off with his thinking about a number of areas he was struggling in and yet hadn't really, openly, truthfully shared any of those struggles with his accountability group. Perhaps you think most people quickly and readily admit when they've got areas that need change. That's not true. Unfortunately, too often they are just like Brian. They may have hurts and challenges that are swamping them emotionally, but they try to put up a front that says, "Nothing's wrong," or they just hint at things that are bothering them.

At The Center for StrongFamilies we teach people about a relationship killer we call "image management." Image management is when we have a public self and a private self, but they're not the same. All of us practice image management to some degree, and in some cases it's absolutely appropriate. For example, have you ever had a rough day and then walked into a restaurant where the table you've been given has the perky waitress or waiter? Let's say this person bounds up to your table and says in that perky voice, "How's it going? Did you have a great day?" In that setting, with a total stranger who isn't really asking to hear about your crummy day, it's totally appropriate to be inauthentic and say, "I'm doing fine." That's because the waitress is just trying to provide a positive atmosphere and perhaps get a bigger tip by being friendly. She's not looking for conversation that's any deeper than, "How's the weather outside?" However, practicing image management with your loved ones or with a small group who genuinely care for you is an invitation for real problems.

If you've had a tough day, it's *not* appropriate to tell people close to you that everything is fine. Certainly, there are timing issues. You don't have to walk in the door and dump all that day's problems on your spouse right when he or she is cooking dinner. But keeping up a false front by using image management to act like everything is great when it really isn't doesn't build relationships. It doesn't allow people to know what's going on inside your heart, and it can set you up for lying and deceiving rather than authenticity and honesty.

As you go through this journal, by yourself or in a small group, here's your chance to say in a safe place what is really going on in your life. It's a safe place to say, "I'm struggling. It's not working. It hasn't been working. I'm afraid. I'm feeling hopeless. I'm in huge trouble."

If you'll think about Brian's story, the issue wasn't where his story started; it was where his small steps took him. The issue isn't where you're starting on this journey; it's where small steps can take you. Has image management been an issue for you in the past? Have you tried to present an "I'm perfect" image to workplace or church friends when you're privately struggling with major issues? The greater the gap we present between who we are and who we say we are, the more at risk we become to the whole deck of cards falling down. For example, 95 percent of the people I work with who have destroyed a marriage because of infidelity struggled with image management. It started with their having a public self that was very different from their private self and continued until the duplicity finally crashed down.

2°

In short, there's no better time than now to be authentic about the changes you need to make. We've all failed and struggled at times. No one is perfect. But a key to change is having the courage to launch into this journal willing to say and share what *is*, not just what you *wish* would be. If you have thoughts or decisions you need to make about exchanging image management for authenticity, then write your thoughts below and pray about sharing them with your small group or a close friend.

_____

_____

_____

Optional Journal Exercise for Those Who Come from a History of Hurt or Failure

Earlier in this journal chapter you were asked to mark whether you felt heartsick or hopeful about the possibilities of change. You were also asked to think back to when you were age ten and mark again if you were heartsick or hopeful as a child. This optional section is a series of thoughts and opportunities that get you to reflect on a key question: Can you really change from being heartsick to hopeful? Or put another way, is there really a way to exchange unhealthy pessimism for genuine optimism, particularly if you've come from a long history of disappointment or discouragement. If you've come from a challenging background, this is one of the most important questions we'll address in the journal.

If you marked yourself as "very hopeful" of making 2 Degree changes as you start this journal, then feel free to skip forward to the next chapter. However, if you come from a difficult background or scored low on this scale (meaning you were skeptical about change), or you live or work closely with someone who did come from a challenging past, then feel free to work through these optional exercises.

For those who want to go deeper still after working through what follows, may I recommend *Breaking the Cycle of Divorce*. While it's a book I wrote specifically for those coming from a difficult past involving divorce, it goes into much greater detail on how you can break negative cycles from all types of difficult backgrounds so that you find yourself on a positive starting point for change.

Let's begin then by first completing an exercise that can help chronicle some of what you've been through. This is an exercise we do with people at The Center for StrongFamilies as a part of a process called LifeMapping that helps people see more clearly where they've been, where they are today, and prayerfully, where they should head in the future.

NOTING THE HIGHPOINT CHALLENGES OF YOUR PAST

Before we talk specifically about whether a person can move from heartsick to hopeful, here's an opportunity to look back at your life story and see just what you've been through—not every challenge, but a way to chronicle some of the key challenges you've faced in the seasons of your life.

Example:

In my early years and teens, three challenges I faced were . . .

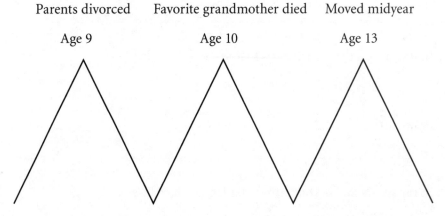

Parents divorced	Favorite grandmother died	Moved midyear
Age 9	Age 10	Age 13

Now it's your turn. As you look at your past, at the top of these three mountain peaks, write down three challenges or difficulties you faced during the time period listed. Feel free to write in initials or to use symbols to stand for something you don't actually want to write out in full if you're concerned about privacy or someone else reading your journal.

Why spend time to focus on these challenges? Because if you're stuck today, a key to moving forward is taking an honest look at what you've been through in the past. For some of you, these challenges will bring back memories, which can bring back feelings, which can bring back more memories. We'll talk about what to do with these hurts and memories shortly and how they may be holding you back from making changes today, but first, take an honest look in the rearview mirror to highlight some of the challenges you've already faced. If you can't come up with three in any one time period, that's fine. Just mark those that surface as significant. If you have more than three in any one time period, then just pick the three *most* difficult that you faced.

In my early years and teens, three challenges I faced were . . .

_____   _____   _____

In my twenties, three challenges I faced were . . .

_____   _____   _____

In my thirties, three challenges I faced were . . .

_____   _____   _____

In my forties, three challenges I faced were . . .

_____   _____   _____

In my fifties, three challenges I faced were . . .

_____   _____   _____

In my sixties and beyond, three challenges I faced were . . .

_____   _____   _____

The exercise above can help you see some of the high-point challenges you've faced in the past. Unfortunately for many people, significant challenges can act like layers of emotional snow and ice during a storm. One storm (or challenge) and the snow and ice can melt fairly quickly once it stops. But add layer after layer of emotional ice like that falling on a mountaintop—or add challenge after challenge to your past—and it can leave a layer of ice that doesn't melt—and a person feeling frozen emotionally.

In *The Lion, the Witch and the Wardrobe*, Lucy found out that all the people living in Narnia were in a land where it was "always winter, but never Christmas." Always cold, yet no calendar certainty that one day the storms would end and be replaced by the warmth and added light of spring. Unfortunately, that's how many people feel who grew up with or have lived through many significant trials. It's like the snow never ends and never will end. But in truth there is something that can generate enough warmth to melt away every layer of ice—not something that will take us back and erase all the hurts that have happened in our past but something that can provide the warmth and light we long for as well as a path down from the cold mountaintops to wide-open spaces. It's the path that even a confirmed pessimist can take to become as optimistic as anyone when it comes to making and keeping 2 Degree changes.

To find this way out of winter, you'll need a Bible, or if you're in a small group, make sure someone has a Bible. Let's start by looking at an example from Scripture that gives us a picture of a person who lived through a difficult past yet shows what happened in her life to put her in position to make real, positive, future-oriented changes.

A Song of Love That Calls Us to a Life of Change

The Song of Songs is the story of two lovers who meet, marry, and provide us with God's picture of "the song of songs," the greatest love story ever lived. Perhaps you'd think that since this is God's picture of an ideal relationship, recorded in his Word for all of history to read, that he would have picked two lovers who were problem free and from wonderful pasts. Actually, God's Word gives us a picture of real life and how real people can live out a song of songs relationship. For the couple pictured in this story grew up in very different backgrounds.

Solomon, the bridegroom, is none other than King David's son. He did, in fact, grow up with a silver spoon, around great wealth, and unlike his father faced few difficult challenges in his early years. Then you've got Solomon's bride. She comes from the kind of "winter storm country" that you did if you listed a great many challenges above. Let's let her tell us about her challenging past and how that froze or stopped her from moving forward in the present.

I am dark, but lovely,

O daughters of Jerusalem,

Like the tents of Kedar,

Like the curtains of Solomon.

Do not stare at me for the sun has burned me.

My mother's sons were angry with me.

They made me care-taker of their vineyard,

I've not been able to take care of my own. (Song 1:5–6)

You learn a great deal about Solomon's bride from this picture she gives us of her background. First, read the verses above once more and then circle *true* or *false* in response to each question.

1. Solomon's bride looks at herself as ugly and unattractive. True or False

2. It was a mark of beauty to be tanned in Solomon's time. True or False

3. You could characterize the "climate" in this woman's home growing up as "sunny and warm." True or False

4. Her brothers made her work hard. True or False

5. Solomon's bride would have been able to take the money she earned from working for her brothers and use this for her dowry when she got married. True or False

Answers: All the answers are false. (Including #4. Read on.)

Let's work through this picture she gives of herself. First, Solomon's bride knows she's pretty. "I am dark but lovely" is how she describes herself. But there's a reason for the dark coloring of her skin that causes her to ask Solomon not to stare at her. She literally says to him, "Turn your eyes away from me!" In short, she's ready to stop this relationship before it starts. That's because when Solomon looks at her, she knows he's going to see her sunburned skin. Far from that being attractive in her day, it was a clear mark that they came from different worlds. He was a king, and she was a working-class woman. As a historical note, there were no "Sinai Sam's Tanning Salons" back in Solomon's day. That's because royalty stayed indoors as much as possible. Being sunburned wasn't considered a mark of beauty. It was the mark of a commoner, a working-class person. So right off, Solomon's bride feels out of her league in her appearance.

Yet it's not just that she came from the wrong side of the working tracks that makes her insecure. She also asks Solomon to turn his eyes from her because she's ashamed of her background.

Was it her brothers that made Solomon's bride work so hard in the vineyards? And was the climate in her home growing up a warm, positive one? No, on both counts. First, these are not her brothers who are making her slave in the sun. Look back at the verses where she describes herself. She calls them her "mother's sons." There is a word for "brothers" in Hebrew, and she chooses not to use that word. Instead, these are angry half or stepbrothers making her work 24-7! (Picture Cinderella, and now you know where that fairy tale was based!) It is these two angry stepbrothers who are making her work full-time in the sun on their vineyards, so she had no time to work on her own. She not only would get nothing for her labors, except shelter and food so she could keep working; but with no harvest of her own, she has no dowry—a terrible thing for a woman who was about to be married in Solomon's day.

In summary then, she's pretty but she's broke, a working-class woman from a challenging background that included a father who had either bailed out on her or died and an angry second family that was robbing her of her future each day. No wonder she looks at Solomon and says, "Turn your eyes away from me." That's what trials do to us. Long-term challenges make us feel that we can't measure up. Trials that seem not to go away can make us feel inside like we're not good enough for the best, like we'll never be good enough. They can leave us feeling that we may as well not even try to be more than we are right at that moment, and so she wants to end the relationship before it begins.

Her insecurity is common enough, but then comes something incredibly uncommon. For in spite of all the emotional storms she'd been through, and the insecurity and hopelessness she felt early on in their relationship, something dramatic changes inside her. Watch this!

Later in the Song of Songs, this is how this same woman describes herself: "I am the rose of Sharon, the lily of the valleys" (Song 2:1).

What a paradigm shift! What an incredible change in how she views herself! And what a huge hint that perhaps there is something that can move us away from being heartsick to hopeful when it comes to change.

For how is it that this woman goes from saying, "Don't look at me!" to "Put me on display!" What changes her mind-set from "I'm not worthy" to feeling that she's the prettiest flower in the entire garden? Not just a rose but *the* rose and *the* lily in fields full of flowers.

In large part this change comes because a very wise Solomon praises his bride more than thirty times in the eight short chapters in this book. In other words, encouragement and praise from a highly valued source (or sources) helps her get a new picture of herself. Genuine praise, affirmation, and encouragement help her change from feeling worthless and hopeless to seeing she has great worth as a person, which in turn blooms out her confidence and changes her view of herself, which should be a strong hint that we need positive people around us and that we should be affirming ourselves.

But in wisdom, Solomon does something else that is crucially important in addition to providing her with a verbally supportive environment.

Solomon asks her to do something that I'm going to ask you to do in a moment if you're serious about change, something you and I particularly will need if either in our past or today change seems hopeless.

The Song of Songs is a book full of metaphors and word pictures. One such metaphor captures a request Solomon makes of his bride before they're married. Solomon calls her thoughts away from home (she was from Lebanon), and away from her past that has been filled with anger and unfairness. He tells her,

> Come with me from Lebanon, my bride,
> May you come with me from Lebanon.
> Journey down from the summit of Amana,
> From the summit of Senir and Hermon,
> From the dens of lions,
> From the mountains of leopards. (Song 4:8)

Let's understand something right off. Amana, Senir, and Hermon aren't old boyfriends he's asking her to forget! ("Forget old Hermon and think about me!"). These are negative high points like those you listed above in each decade of your life. Solomon's use of "high peaks" and summits wasn't intended to create images of grandeur or security. Desert dwellers of his day didn't look at mountain peaks the way X-Games athletes or extreme skiers look at snowcapped summits today—with optimism and enthusiasm. Mountain peaks were seen as places of fear and even danger. Note, too, that Solomon tosses in lions and leopards as well to highlight the fear factor. In other words, Solomon is asking his bride to move away from all those fearful high points in her past, to move away from all the things she would have listed in the charts above as you did. He calls her to come down from them as a first step toward their connecting in a new life in the present.

While you really need to read an outstanding commentary on the Song of Songs to unpack all the metaphors in this book completely (I like *Solomon's Song of Love* by S. Craig Glickman, Ph.D.), in short here's what's being pictured. And here too is why looking at this bride and her husband is so important to you and me when it comes to making small changes—just in case you were wondering about the connection.

Solomon asks in a poetic way for his bride to leave behind all those challenging times filled with fear and unrest. In many ways Solomon's request is a living picture of the words in Genesis 2:24, "For this reason a man shall leave his father and his mother, and be joined to his wife."

It was only after Solomon's bride did just this that she saw her life bloom as never before. Only when she moved *toward* him and *away from* her fearful, hurtful past, did her view of herself begin to change. And there's a reason her moving *toward* her bridegroom had such an impact on the hurt she'd suffered.

Think for a moment about how moving *toward* someone who is affirming and supportive can impact another person's life, even if that person has come from a difficult background. The fact is, there is tremendous power in love to heal, to restore, and to reframe a person's view of himself or herself. It's what you've seen in movies for years when a rough-edged character falls in love and begins to change. It's Beauty and the Beast. It's Jack Nicholson saying in *As Good as It Gets,* "You make me want to be a better man."

Now think about this. Jesus' love for us is addressed at length in Ephesians 5, and guess how our relationship with him is described? The church is pictured as his "bride," and his commitment to it is to present her whole and spotless and complete to his Father.

Do you get the picture?

2°

In the Song of Songs, a woman from a hurtful past is called on by her husband to let his love renew and restore her. It's when she takes those steps toward her beloved that she begins to move internally from feeling like a weed to a rose. That's the picture of our relationship with Christ. Solomon may have been the wisest man on earth for a time, but if you know anything about his later life, he ended up failing to follow God's or his own advice. (Read the book of Ecclesiastes to learn how he realizes life apart from God is "vanity" and his conclusion that he should have never walked away.)

Jesus, our Bridegroom, is the same yesterday, today, and forever. He never changes. He never stops loving you. He never stops calling you and me to come away from the scary places and difficult times in our past. He never stops reaching out a nail-scarred hand to pull us out of an impossible situation. God's love poured through Jesus can make us whole, complete, and spotless; it can make us blossom like the prettiest rose.

That is a huge starting-point truth as we begin our look at making 2 Degree changes. By leaving past hurts and cleaving to the lover of our soul—Jesus—we can see ourselves become whole and complete. We can gain forgiveness for past wrongs we've done, and we can quit trafficking in guilt and self-condemnation. We're told in God's Word, "There is now no condemnation for those who are in Christ Jesus" (Romans 8:1). The focus shifts from us trying to be more, do more, be perfect, regain what we've lost, which we either can't or never will, to the freedom of taking his hand and taking those small steps of faith and love.

If we're serious about making positive changes today, that call to move away from past hurts and toward someone who can change our heart and life is real, and it's the only lasting answer to the question, Can you change from being heartsick to hopeful? And then this brings us to another question.

For you personally, has there been a time in your life when you've asked Jesus, God's own Son, to come into your life to be your Savior and Lord? Has there been a time when you reached out your hand, took his nail-scarred hand, and came away with him as he's drawn you away from all the hurt and pain in the past? Have you accepted the incredible love and healing and newness of life Jesus offers? If you have, describe such a time in your life and what truly believing in Jesus has done for you. And if you honestly *can't* say there's ever been a specific time when you've reached out your hand to take Jesus' hand, then skip down to the question below . . .

_____

_____

_____

_____

_____

_____

If you've never reached out and taken Jesus' hand, why not right now? Jesus gave his disciples a "picture" of how he loved them in this way, "Behold, I stand at the door and knock; if anyone . . . opens the door, I will come in to him and will dine with him, and he with Me" (Revelation 3:20). That's a picture of what you can have in a personal relationship with Jesus. Here is someone who actively initiates a loving relationship with us. He knocks on our door—a real, living person named Jesus whose love is strong enough to lift you and me out of all the hurt and put our feet on solid ground. Jesus the Bridegroom offers his hand to you right now. And all you need to do is open the door of your heart. There's no handle on the outside, just on the inside. Recognize and admit your need of God's Son, who can do for you what you can't do for yourself. Reach out to the only One who can forgive you of your sins and wrongs in the past and provide you with a new life starting today, this moment.

If you think about it, there are few "do-overs" in life, yet one is being offered to you right now. God's Word says, "Today is the 'day of salvation'" Today is the day we need to respond. It also says, "If any man be in Christ, he is a new creature. Old things are passed away. Behold all things have become new."

Here's your chance to let all those old hurts and scary things you charted earlier become empty shadows of your past. All it takes is reaching out your hand and taking Jesus' hand in faith. And when you do, we're told, "Whoever believes in Him shall not perish, but have eternal life"

(John 3:16). Coming to Christ gives you new life today and an eternity with him tomorrow. Accepting Jesus gives you a new family to love you (his church) and a book filled with affirming words on how much he cares for you (the Bible) and guidance 24/7 to become the whole, positive person you can become. Like a bride accepting her bridegroom's hand, you get an uplifting, energizing, redemptive, intimate relationship with Jesus, the only One powerful enough to give you the "newness of life" you've wanted and waited for so long.

If you're ready to make that decision and reach out and take his hand right now, then in your own way reach out your hand to accept his. Some people find it helpful to pray a prayer like, "Thank you, Jesus, for knowing me and all my faults and failures, yet still loving me unconditionally. Thank you for calling me away from the scary places and past hurts, to a life with you. Please forgive me for all my falling short, and thank you for taking my hand today and forever. Amen."

If you prayed such a prayer, be sure you write down the day and date and in your own words the decision you just made as you spoke that prayer. You'll want to write down the where and when of this decision because while you may not hear them as you write the words, angels in heaven were singing because you prayed that prayer. For one that was lost is found, and one who was in darkness has found a great light.

If in fact you are a "new creature," does that mean you don't need all this *2 Degree Difference* talk from now on? Can't you just close the book, walk away from your small group, and go out now and do everything differently?

While in a relationship with Christ you do have everything you need to live a life of love and godliness, guess what? As a new believer, the Bible pictures your spiritual life like that of a newborn baby. Babies need milk, which we're told is God's Word, and constant attention, which is what God's Holy Spirit will begin to do inside you now and a good church can help provide as well; and of course there is no substitute for time to grow and mature. And that's why you need to go through the rest of this workbook.

If you remember, Brian's problem wasn't that he didn't know Jesus. Brian went to church conferences, joined campaigns, read spiritual books, prayed time and again, and even typed out his purpose statement. Yet nothing seemed to change, and he didn't feel like his life had become any more purposeful or positive at all. Why? In large part it was because he kept doing what has kept people in every generation from moving forward. Brian thought if he just did enough big things in his life and faith, he'd get the big results he wanted.

What Brian had to learn from Eric and from reading God's Word—and what you now know from reading Brian's story—is that it wasn't the big things but being faithful in a little that would bring great change, 2 Degree changes, one-inch changes. The kind you're ready to keep reading and talking about.

You're ready now to keep moving forward in the journal to chapter 2. Admittedly, over the next several chapters, we'll see more of what didn't work in Brian's life than what did. But keep in mind that you know the score at the end of the game when it comes to Brian's life. He may be struggling now, but he'll soon learn about the kind of small things that will get him on the winning side.

waking up to an unwanted reality

In this first glimpse of Brian's life, he gets a major wake-up call that not only erases a wonderful dream but replaces it with an unwanted reality. That's what we'll focus on in this second journal chapter, that gap between who we are really and the person we wish we were or could be.

For Brian, slipping into a dream based on the dime-store Western novel created a razor-sharp contrast with the reality he was facing at home. Take just a moment to look back through the story of the sheriff. As you look at the picture portrayed in this Old West scene, what character traits or other personal elements surface that you feel might have reflected unmet needs or wishes in Brian's life?

_____

_____

_____

_____

_____

Looking in the other direction, when Brian woke up (thanks to the flight attendant), reality was something very different from his dreams. What are some of the obvious things and, looking more closely, some of the more subtle parts of Brian's real life that contrasted with the picture of that sheriff in his dreams?

_____

_____

_____

_____

Let's reflect for a moment on wake-up calls. Brian's story highlights several common areas where people have their eyes opened to the fact that things aren't the way they want them to be. And we'll see there are several issues and areas in Brian's life that didn't match up with the man he wants to see in his dreams. While we'll go into several of those in the next chapter, for now, have you personally ever had a real-life wake-up call in some area of your life? If so, list that area and what woke you up to the fact that there was a gap between the way you thought things were and what reality revealed.

_____

_____

_____

_____

_____

_____

Unfortunately, emotional wake-up calls are almost always negative. For example, what's more common? To stand in front of the mirror and say, "Look at you! You have _got_ to lose weight and start exercising right now!" or "Amazing! You look great! You've lost so much weight!" Whether it's our health or our home or even our heart for God, there are times in our life when we'll get a wake-up call that things aren't what they should be.

It is common for humans like us to have our eyes opened to the fact that we're not where we want to be or perhaps ever thought we'd be. You were asked earlier to identify one area in your life where you received a wake-up call. If you couldn't think of a single area where your eyes have been opened to a gap between where you are and where you want to be, then think about those three areas just mentioned—your health, home, or your heart for God. Take any one of the three and either personally, or in people you've seen, describe what a person's most common reaction is when he or she first gets that wake-up call.

Example, wake-up call: Someone goes to the doctor and hears that his health is so bad that he's at risk of a major medical meltdown.

Reaction: He immediately goes on an "I'll never eat a single bad thing ever" diet.

Your example, wake-up call: _____

_____

Reaction: _____

_____

_____

_____

In most cases, when we or when someone we know gets a wake-up call, it draws forth an almost instantaneous reaction to do something big, dramatic, extraordinary—meaning anything except what's been ordinary for us. As a rule, we simply don't think "small things" when large gaps appear.

In the next journal chapter we'll look more closely at several areas in Brian's life where gaps appeared between his dreams and reality. But for now let's look at someone else who awoke to an unwanted reality.

How Looking at Two Charcoal Fires Can Open Your Eyes to Wake-Up Calls

There once was a man who was fast asleep, like Brian. Only he wasn't on an airplane. He was in a hillside garden, and it was late at night. While we don't know what Peter was dreaming, he was definitely asleep when

Jesus woke him up in Gethsemane. In fact, Jesus woke him up three times.

If you recall the story, Jesus had taken only his closest friends to a secluded garden to pray about the terrible things that lay ahead of him—unlawful arrest, false trials, scourging, mocking, and finally crucifixion. Jesus knew all of this was facing him; and he wanted, asked, almost begged for help from his closest friends in these most terrible hours. The hours before battle are indeed terrible, and the last thing you want is to be alone. But three times when Jesus went a short distance away to pray, Peter, James, and John fell asleep instead of staying up to support Jesus. And the final time Jesus woke up Peter and the others, it was to show them the lights of the many torches coming up the steep slope to the garden, torches carried by temple guards led by Judas coming to arrest Jesus.

If you're familiar with this story of Jesus' praying to his Father and his betrayal at the hands of Judas, then you'll most likely remember something else as well. It's what happened earlier that same evening when Jesus and his disciples had shared the Passover meal together. There at the meal Jesus told his closest followers that one of them, seated at that table, would betray him. (See Matthew 26 for the whole story.) There at the meal Jesus told them that he would soon be arrested and killed, and they would all scatter in fear when it happened.

Do you remember what Peter told Jesus in response?

"But Peter said to Him, 'Even though all may fall away because of You, I will never fall away'" (Matthew 26:33).

And if you'll recall Jesus' answer to Peter's boast, it was to tell him that before the morning came, he would deny him three times. Peter's response was even more dramatic to Christ's suggestion that he'd fail him that night or any other.

"Peter said to Him, 'Even if I have to die with You, I will not deny You'" (Matthew 26:35).

Remember, we're talking about wake-up calls in this journal chapter. Peter was only hours away from getting an incredibly dramatic wake-up call that has a great deal to teach us about wake-up calls of our own as well.

The First of Two Charcoal Fires

Keep your eyes open for charcoal fires as this wake-up call story unfolds. They play a key role in what happens with Peter and in what can happen in your life if you get a wake-up call.

Even though Peter did make a feeble attempt to resist when Judas and the soldiers came up to arrest Jesus, he quickly ran away like all the others. But Peter didn't run far away. In fact, Peter ended up following the mob as they took Jesus to the house of the high priest.

While Jesus was being questioned inside, Peter actually came into the high priest's courtyard. It was cold outside—a bitter cold, high-desert evening there in Jerusalem. What drew Peter to that house was to see what was happening with Jesus. But what drew him into the very courtyard where Jesus was being questioned was a charcoal fire that had been built to warm those who were up so late that night.

While Peter stood over this first charcoal fire, a young servant girl confronted him, asking him if he was one of Jesus' followers. For the first time, Peter denied knowing Jesus. Then another man standing around the fire questioned Peter, and he made the second denial. And when others joined in, certain that he was one of Jesus' disciples, Peter denied it a third time, this time lacing his answer with swearing and cursing.

The Gospel of Luke then gives us one of the most heart-wrenching pictures of a wake-up call imaginable. Remember, Peter swore he would never leave Jesus, that he would never deny Christ. Now he's run away and denied Jesus three times. And then Dr. Luke describes what happened this way: "The Lord turned and looked at Peter. And Peter remembered the word of the Lord, how He had told him, 'Before a rooster crows today, you will deny Me three times.' And he [Peter] went out and wept bitterly" (Luke 22:61–62).

Can you imagine looking into Jesus' eyes at that moment? That's the wake-up call Peter got that showed him clearly there was a huge gap between who he may have dreamed about being and who he really was at that time. It's like Brian waking up on the airplane and realizing his life was a wreck. And it was also the first time the Bible tells us Peter stood over a charcoal fire.

2°

If you've had a wake-up call lately or in the past, you're in good company. But keep in mind that it isn't having a wake-up call that's the issue. It's what you do when it comes. In Peter's case, let's look at what Jesus does that makes all the difference.

The Second Charcoal Fire

There was a second time that Peter stood over a charcoal fire. In fact, in all the New Testament, there are only two times when the word *charcoal* is used. Once is in the Gospel of John (chapter 19) when Peter is standing over a charcoal fire and denied Jesus. And then there's one other time after Jesus had risen from the grave and appeared to the disciples. You can read the story in detail in John 21.

Peter had already seen the risen Lord Jesus. However, it's clear things simply weren't the same. Think of how you'd feel if you were now around someone you loved deeply but had betrayed so dramatically. So Peter decided that if he'd failed so badly at being a rock-solid disciple, then at least he could go back to doing something he was good at—fishing.

Fishing was Peter's vocation before he was a disciple. In fact, that's what Peter had been doing the first time he ever saw Jesus. The first time Peter met Jesus, he, his brother, and their crew had been out all night fishing and caught nothing. Now it was morning; they had washed out their nets for the next day and were putting them away in their boat. A huge crowd had gathered and was milling around near where they'd grounded their boat. People from everywhere were waiting to hear from Jesus.

Because the wide sloped beach where they'd run up their boat made a perfect natural amphitheater, Jesus walked right up to Peter and asked if he could use his boat to teach the crowd. Peter agreed. They pushed out a short way so that people could sit down on the sand. Jesus shared with them and with those listening on the boat. When his message concluded, he asked Peter to push out to sea and put down his nets to make a catch.

Peter had fished all night the night before and caught nothing. His nets were already cleaned, stored, and ready for the next day. He told this to Jesus; but seeing his guests' insistence and wanting to honor or not wanting to embarrass his guest (or perhaps *wanting* to when they caught nothing and he could say, "I told you so!"), Peter pushed out to deeper water and put down his nets. Immediately he caught so many fish that his net filled and his boat began to sink.

Peter called to another fishing boat to come and help, and *their* nets filled up immediately with so many fish that *both* boats were nearly pulled under.

Peter has fished all his life, and he knows such things don't happen, and then he suddenly understands why it is happening. It's because of who is in his boat. And with that understanding, instantly "he fell down at Jesus' feet, saying, 'Go away from me Lord, for I am a sinful man.' For amazement had seized him and all his companions because of the catch of fish which they had taken" (Luke 5:8–9).

That was the first time Peter met Jesus, and it's when Jesus called Peter to be a "fisher of men." Peter left everything that day to follow Jesus. And then came the night when "The Rock" (the name Jesus had given him) stood over that charcoal fire and three times denied he even knew Jesus.

That's why Peter went back to something he did well—fishing. Accompanied by several of the other disciples, he fished all night and caught nothing. But early the next morning, as they neared shore, they saw someone on the shore. He called to them and said, "You haven't caught anything, have you." Think about that for a moment. It's not a question, and it doesn't sound all that positive. A positive thing to say would have been, "Caught anything?" Instead, "You haven't caught anything, have you" is a statement that's close to fighting words for some. But it's not a fight Jesus is looking for with Peter; it's to put the fight back in him.

This man sitting on the beach told those in the boat to put down their nets for a catch. When they did, it was an instant replay of the first time Peter met Jesus. So many fish filled their nets and boat that it was on the edge of capsizing. And that's when the "beloved disciple" John recognized and alerted the others that Jesus was standing on the beach. Peter didn't even wait for them to land their boat. He jumped in the water and swam to shore and came and stood beside Jesus. And now let's pick up the story in Scripture: "So when they got out on the land, they saw a charcoal fire, already laid and fish placed on it, and bread" (John 21:9).

Here then at this second charcoal fire that Jesus built, Peter was invited to stand. Remember, only twice in all the New Testament do you find the word *charcoal*. Both are in the Gospel of John: first when Peter denied Jesus three times and this time, when Jesus asked Peter three times, "Do you love me?"

It's an amazing replay for Peter. He'd just seen Jesus do the same miracle he did when they first met. The message from that miracle is clear. Nothing in who Jesus is had changed a bit since that first day Peter fell at his feet and called him Lord. Jesus is the same yesterday, today, and forever.

But Peter has changed. Peter woke up to the fact that he'd fallen short.

Peter had changed since he denied Christ three times. But Jesus repeated that miracle of the fish not only to show Peter that who he is hadn't changed but also to show Peter who he can be hadn't changed either.

Three times, that morning on the beach, Jesus asked Peter, "Do you love me?" Each time, once for each denial, Peter told the Lord, "Yes."

And what then did Jesus ask of Peter?

He'd failed big time. Right?

So to make things right between them, Jesus asked Peter to do something big to get back on track. Right? I think by this stage in the book, you already know the answer, and it's not that Jesus asked him to do some great thing.

"Do you love me?" Jesus asked.

"Yes, Lord, you know I love you," Peter replied.

"Then tend my lambs."

"Shepherd my sheep."

"Tend my sheep."

Jesus told Peter to go back to being a servant of his people, to do the small things it takes to be a servant or a shepherd. To take one child in his arms, one of his little lambs. To serve his people. To tend his sheep.

Let's make that long story short and personal as we continue to look at making 2 Degree changes. When Peter was shown to have a great gap between who he may have dreamed or said he was to others and who he actually was when the chips were down, Jesus sat him down and set him straight. The thing that would close the gap between the person Peter thought or wanted to be and who he was, first and foremost sitting next to Jesus and knowing he was still loved, and then living out that love in small ways. "Tend my lambs."

In the last chapter, if you did the optional exercise, you saw that love— God's love—has the power to heal past hurts. Here love again causes gaps to close; God's love accepted and small acts of love lived out will change Brian's life just as it did Peter's.

What are your thoughts about this story from Scripture? What do you think about the way Jesus dealt with Peter? If there are gaps between who you are and who you want to be or feel you should be, do you believe it will be big things or small acts that will close that gap? Share your thoughts below and with your small group or a close friend on the story of two charcoal fires and on small loving acts and change.

_____

_____

_____

_____

_____

_____

_____

2°

how low can you go?

Things certainly went from bad to worse for Brian in this chapter. Here's how it's stated in chapter 3:

> Brian's dream had been filled with pictures of courage, strength, and clear convictions. Images still lingered of a warm family relationship and of a man who had an overwhelming sense of a job and life well-done. Now, as he forced himself to stare out the window, Brian felt simply overwhelmed. Instead of a whole town looking up to him, Brian felt incredibly alone and about as valuable to anyone as a used-up, twisted-up, discarded dishrag. It wasn't for any lack of effort, he knew; but it seemed like the very things most important to him were slipping away, and there was nothing he could do about it.

Overwhelmed is perhaps an understatement for the way Brian felt. Instead of a whole town looking up to him, he felt more like a poster child for "what *not* to do" when it came to living out a life of courage, purpose, and fulfillment. In this journal chapter, let's look at the key areas where Brian began to come to grips with the gaps between who was and the person he should be or could be.

Please keep one thing in mind: For most of us, like Brian, when it rains, it pours.

It would be wonderful if life came at us just one thing at a time. Wouldn't it be great if only one area of our life was allowed to demand our attention or to beg for change at a time? Then we could race over, patch any cracks, and then rest and wait for the next area that was patiently waiting its turn to show a weakness or struggle. That's not real life. For most of us, trials and demands in our lives come in waves. For Brian, there were simply too many holes in the dike for all his fingers and toes to reach, and they all were leaking at once.

It's this axiom of life that can make things seem so challenging when it comes to change. It is also another powerful reason 2 Degree changes are so important. When we have multiple areas we need to work on—health, home, work, extended family—it can seem like working on just one area *isn't* going to help, so we often don't do anything at all. Either that, or we feel like we need to work on everything, in big ways, right now—and get little done in any one area.

That is exactly why *2 Degree Differences* can make such a positive difference in our life. Remember, change in one area grows at *compound interest.* Making small changes in one area of life actually provides spill-over gains in many other areas of our life. While there may not be a parallel for that at your local bank (where interest in one account lifts all your accounts), you can take to the bank that small changes in one area will help you in a widespread way throughout your life.

But before we jump ahead to making those small changes, we need to take an important next step to do purposefully what Brian does accidentally on the plane. If you'll remember, in his mind's eye, Brian pictured a large sheet of paper and himself holding a large, black permanent marker. As he goes through the major areas of his life, it's like he checking off success or failure in area after area. Hopefully, you'll find few areas where you feel like you're on the bubble or where things seem to be coming apart, as they were for Brian. However, let's look at each of the major, common areas of life where Brian saw a significant gap between where he was and where he wanted to be and apply this to our lives as well.

Here's another place where you don't want to practice image management as we defined it earlier. Instead of worrying about your image, concentrate on being honest as you work through the major life areas listed below. We'll go in the same order that Brian checks off his list, plus give you a chance to add another area not listed that's a plate you're spinning.

Feel free to skip over issues or areas that don't apply in your unique life setting.

Walking through Our Life Story

IN THE WORKPLACE

If you're working, how do you feel about your job and the way things are progressing at your workplace, relative to where you know deep inside you should be? Give yourself a numerical rating (instead of Brian's "failure" or "success" checkmark), and then explain why you chose the number you did.

In the Workplace

1	2	3	4	5	6	7

Not doing or finding the
degree of success I feel I should

Doing great
in this area

Explain why you chose the number you did.

_____

_____

_____

_____

_____

_____

_____

_____

2°

IN SIGNIFICANT RELATIONSHIPS

If you're married, engaged, or seriously dating, how do you feel your relationship is going relative to where you want it to be?

In My Marriage or with My Fiancé

1	2	3	4	5	6	7

Not doing or finding the
degree of success I feel I should

Doing great
in this area

Explain why you chose the number you did.

_____

_____

_____

_____

_____

_____

WITH MY CHILDREN

If you've got kids of any age, how do you feel your relationship is right now with your child(ren) in terms of it being where you want it to be?

As a Parent

1	2	3	4	5	6	7

Not doing or finding the
degree of success I feel I should

Doing great
in this area

Explain why you chose the number you did.

_____

_____

_____

_____

_____

In Your Spiritual Life and Faith

In your faith, how do you feel you're doing relative to where you want to be or feel you should be?

In Your Faith and Spiritual Life

1	2	3	4	5	6	7

Not doing or finding the
degree of success I feel I should

Doing great
in this area

Explain why you chose the number you did.

_____

_____

_____

In Your Health

In your health, how do you feel you're doing when it comes to being healthy, physically and emotionally, compared to where you feel you need to be?

In My Health

1	2	3	4	5	6	7

Not doing or finding the
degree of success I feel I should

Doing great
in this area

Explain why you chose the number you did.

_____

_____

2°

_____

_____

_____

AN AREA OF LIFE UNIQUE TO YOU

Is there an area in your life (dealing with in-laws, building solid friendships, finances, volunteer activities, etc.) that isn't listed above that you need to add to your personal checklist?

This Area Is _____

1	2	3	4	5	6	7

Not doing or finding the   Doing great
degree of success I feel I should   in this area

Explain why you chose the number you did.

_____

_____

_____

_____

_____

_____

Please remember: The issue isn't where you are _today_ on any of these life-role areas. It's where small steps, prayerfully made, can take you in the days to come. Just for taking the time and effort to work through the list above, give yourself a hug or a warm pat on the back for going through the kind of mental, emotional, spiritual, and physical checkup that Brian went through on the plane. For Brian, it was more of an accidental checklist brought on by the wake-up call he received on the plane. However, I think it's even more important for people volitionally and purposefully to take an honest look at their life story.

Unfortunately, most people are so caught up in the tyranny of the urgent that they never stop to reflect on where they are today or could or should be tomorrow. That's why the average person skips their annual physical: they're too busy with today's trials to do something proactive. And what's more, there's the real fear that if the doctor *does* find something wrong, then they don't have the time or energy to confront it! You're far wiser than most people for completing the evaluation above and doing an honest self-reflection checkup. In fact, here's how God's Word describes what you've taken the time to do: "Behold, You [God] desire truth in the innermost being, and in the hidden part You will make me know wisdom" (Psalm 51:6). God's Word also says, "How much better it is to get wisdom then gold! And to get understanding is to be chosen above silver" (Proverbs 16:16).

And to quote just one more reason Almighty God values so highly the kind of honest searching and knowing of yourself you've just done, listen to this benefit of taking the time to reflect closely on where you are today and should be tomorrow. "The wisdom of the wise keeps life on track; the foolishness of fools lands them in the ditch" (Proverbs 14:8 *The Message*). That's a message from Almighty God that's worth memorizing and keeping in mind each day as you begin the process of making 2 Degree changes.

We'll come back to your answers on these various life areas and how 2 Degree changes can help you close any gaps, but let's look at two more things from this chapter before we move away from reflection and on to everyday action.

How Low Can You Go?

The title of this chapter "How Low Can You Go?" was picked on purpose. If you remember from this chapter, there was a time on the descent into Denver when Brian's fear factor went way up. It happened when the plane hit a double dose of turbulence. Flying into Denver, there is normally a degree of turbulence as you hit the air thermals coming off the mountains. But in this case the normal light chop was linked with a thunderstorm in the area that not only gave Brian a bump on the head but made him think about his mortality as well.

Here's another place where I'm going to ask you to be brutally honest with yourself, as Brian was that night on the plane. After cycling through all the life areas listed above where Brian didn't feel he was doing well, the turbulence surrounding the plane caused Brian to have one of those "George Bailey/*It's a Wonderful Life*" moments. Namely, Brian felt so overwhelmed with all the *negative checkmarks* he had given himself, so discouraged that all his efforts had seemed to be either unnoticed or unrewarded, so tired of trying not to compare what he had or had not done with others he perceived as more successful that he was at the point of despairing of life. For just a moment, if you remember, Brian actually pondered that if the plane went down, perhaps that would be a better alternative for his family. It was only a thought, quickly dispelled, but it wasn't put in this chapter accidentally. Did you know that even great saints, when they reached the end of their rope and felt overwhelmed by all the challenges and trials in front of them, actually felt for a moment like Brian?

"For we do not want you to be unaware, brethren, of our affliction which came *to us* in Asia, that we were burdened excessively, beyond our strength, so that we despaired even of life" (2 Corinthians 1:8). That's the apostle Paul speaking.

Or how about these words from Elijah: "But he himself went a day's journey into the wilderness, and came and sat down under a juniper tree; and he requested for himself that he might die, and said, 'It is enough; now, O LORD, take my life, for I am not better than my fathers,'" (1 Kings 19:4).

Obviously, these must be words from two faithless, minor characters in the Bible, right? Try instead, they are the words of the apostle Paul (2 Corinthians 1:8) and the mighty prophet Elijah (1 Kings 19:4). Both of these giants of the faith came to such a low place in their lives that they reached the same emotional conclusion as George Bailey in *It's a Wonderful Life* would centuries later. After all their efforts, both Paul and Elijah saw their problems as so big, the options for change so few, that they thought perhaps they'd be better off just going to heaven and leaving all the struggles behind.

I share that with you because it's important to do two things. First, realize that if you've checked off a series of low numbers in those major life areas above, you're not alone if you've gotten so discouraged that for a fleeting moment, things seemed like they'd only get better if you weren't around. The truth is that for Paul, Elijah, Brian, me, or anyone, acting on those feelings when we feel so lonely or overburdened doesn't solve anything and never will. In fact, it *creates* far more problems than it can ever solve. Go back to George Bailey and the story I know you know so well in *It's a Wonderful Life* (and yes, I know he's an imaginary character). While I seriously doubt that your guardian angel is named Clarence, angels are real, and they are just one of the countless ways Almighty God can break through to us and remind us that life is *always* worth living. Believe it or not, 99.9 percent of people who drown do so within ten feet of shore. There's no reason—even thinking that "things would be better without me"—for giving up and acting on such negative feelings. But there's also no reason for hating yourself or feeling you're the only one who has ever felt that the challenges you face are almost too much to carry.

Remember that Brian's story, if only looked at from that one snapshot moment on the plane, seemed to him to be hopeless. It may have been on the plane, but it wasn't in reality. Hope was right around the corner, or in his case, just a coffee shop meeting and an e-mail from his son away. I'm not sure what the Lord has in mind to remind you of his faithfulness (as he did with Paul, Elijah, Brian, me, and so many others). Perhaps it's the encouragement you'll get from your small group if you're working through this book with a band of brothers or sisters. Or perhaps it's knowing that God's Spirit can encourage you to stay the course through passages like this:

> Why do you say, O Jacob, and assert, O Israel,
> "My way is hidden from the LORD,
> And the justice due me escapes the notice of my God"?
> Do you not know? Have you not heard?
> The Everlasting God, the LORD, the Creator of the ends of the earth
> Does not become weary or tired.
> His understanding is inscrutable.
> He gives strength to the weary,

And to him who lacks might He increases power.

Though youths grow weary and tired,

And vigorous young men stumble badly,

Yet those who wait for the LORD

Will gain new strength;

They will mount up with wings like eagles,

They will run and not get tired,

They will walk and not become weary. (Isaiah 40:27–31)

Don't give up whatever you've marked above or whatever you feel today. God can and does give help and strength and hope to those who are weary and tired. Even the strongest among us stumble, sometimes badly. But the key is knowing that Almighty God can and does bring us life, hope, encouragement, love, friends, and everything else we need to soar, run, and walk toward a God-honoring future.

If you're in a small group, discuss your thoughts on the section above. If you're working through this journal on your own, what are your thoughts after having read the above?

_____

_____

_____

_____

_____

_____

A First Look at Brian's Remedy of Choice—Big Problems, Big Campaigns

As Brian went through his laundry list of issues and areas he needed to work on, we also get our first look at what he had relied on in the past to pull himself out of the challenges before him.

Campaigns. Conferences. Books. Challenges. Commitments.
Countless prayers. For almost three decades, Brian had been there, done
that, gotten the T-shirt, and then gone back to get the alumni and volunteer T-shirts. All of these things had helped Brian when he was right
in the midst of a packed stadium or sitting in a crowded pew at church
on Sunday. But somehow, between walking out of a stadium or sanctuary and reaching his car, it was like something crucial evaporated
inside him.

Because this will show up prominently in the next journal chapter,
we'll discuss this idea of "big problems, big campaigns" in the next chapter. But I wanted to remind you of the quote above because of its contrast
with one last image from this chapter.

It's the little thing that was the last straw for Brian.

In case you missed it, read again at the very end of the chapter how
Brian's plane flight ended. Do you remember how it looked like rain was
coming in from outside the plane, soaking his briefcase, and how it ended
up that Brian had put a nearly full can of Diet Coke in the seat pocket in
front of him?

I share this because in my counseling practice I have seen time and
again that the last straw is often something incredibly small in comparison
to all that's happened in the past. It's like a couple fighting hard to keep
their marriage together after a season of major challenges, and then one
of them squeezing the toothpaste tube the wrong way becomes such a big
deal that it convinces the other person that all their efforts are worthless.
Or it's that one small argument on the way to church that convinces someone that they'll never go back again. Here in Brian's story, it's something
small and admittedly unwise, like spilling a soda can, that seemed like
the last nail on the coffin for Brian. When he saw the mess at his feet, it
became emblematic of his whole life. It wasn't just a failure to dispose of
a can of Diet Coke; it was certain confirmation that his life was a failure
and he was an idiot on top of being a failure.

That final straw picture was a part of the "low as you can go" look
at his life, a small thing that acted almost like a magnet, drawing and
reflecting all the big problems around him as insurmountable.

Honestly, have you ever felt that way? Have you ever had a small issue become so big that it became a thousand-pound weight instead of a seven-ounce tube of toothpaste? For Brian, that spilled diet soda should have been upsetting but not overwhelming.

One more time, in your small group or here in the journal on your own, take time to answer a question: Has there been a time in your life when a small thing became a picture of everything that is wrong? If so, then jot down your thoughts below, or talk about it with your friends, and ask Almighty God to help you put in perspective that toothpaste tube or diet soda can, or your last straw. And if not, then keep this insight in mind for some time down the road when a small thing can seem like everything is wrong. For it's the little things that can prove powerfully negative in our lives if we're not careful.

Write about your thoughts on a small thing representing a huge thing.

_____

_____

_____

_____

_____

_____

_____

when things just can't get any worse

I t may seem like piling on, but once again we're looking at Brian's life story; and what we see are things getting worse, not better. As you know, life does get better for Brian, but at this point he still has a few more challenges ahead of him. His issues point out important things for us to discuss in this journal chapter.

If you're in a small group, or if you're not now but have been in a small group, what's your experience been with groups in the past? Positive? Negative? Explain your thoughts and experience.

_____

_____

_____

_____

_____

Who is a person in your life who reminds you of Eric? Someone who may be a little unconventional, like an aunt who always dressed funny and perhaps was a little loud in public but who always loved you deeply and told you the truth even when you didn't want to hear it. What's so powerful about an "Eric" type friend or family member? What would it take for you to be an "Eric" to someone else? Discuss and jot down your answers to these questions.

_____

_____

_____

_____

_____

Let's take a look at Brian's reactions to two different stimuli. The first was the dreaded mirror. In chapter 4 we read:

> Brian struggled to reach over and place the phone back in its cradle on the nightstand next to the bed. Then he gave a sigh and willed himself to get out of bed. As he walked past the large mirror on the wall, he caught a glimpse of himself in the XXL T-shirt and running shorts he used for pajamas. One look made him think for a moment about exercising. He should do at least a few sit-ups or push-ups. But then came all the rationalizations. After all, he had already missed his meeting. And he really did need to get in to work. He could exercise tomorrow maybe. After winning (or losing) the "I need to exercise" battle, he walked to the kitchen, opened the refrigerator, and pulled out several toaster waffles.

One reason Brian struggled with exercise is captured in this description. Read through his thought process again and ask and answer below how much it's like your own. If you've struggled in this area of consistent exercise, how does thinking about "everything on your plate" for the rest of the day influence what you do that morning? Think in particular about big challenges and 2 Degree investments of time as you do so.

_____

_____

_____

Yet another area where Brian struggled was linking comfort food to emotional challenges. Here's a picture of that from chapter 4:

> He [Brian] didn't feel a bit hungry anymore. Still, he stayed in the kitchen and ate two toaster waffles. Then he went back and got a third. Each one he layered with butter and then drenched with syrup. If he'd thought about it, eating alone and eating food covered in syrup or sauce was more and more becoming his reaction of choice to feeling emotionally like another door had been slammed in his face.

How strong of a pull does comfort food have on you as you face challenges in your life and relationships? Break down why that connection can be so strong and so difficult to break. What is there about the *2 Degree Difference* that can be misused when it comes to food, remembering that good and bad acts can grow at compound interest?

From Challenges at Home to Major Challenges in His Workplace

Have you ever worked for someone like "The Bulldog" whom Brian had to report to each week? What is it about having to be constantly under a challenging person like that, that seems to add numerous "degree of difficulty" points to everything we do at work? How can a non-affirming, demanding person punch holes in any big plans we have for change?

_____

_____

_____

_____

_____

_____

_____

The probation letter that Brian received was a long list of areas in which he would have to make major changes if he was to keep his job. When the solution we're given to a problem is an arm-long list, it's common to think what Brian did: "*Another list*, he thought to himself. Another chance at the end for him to check 'failure' next to these huge tasks he knew were next to impossible to meet."

Have you ever felt that between you and success, or just staying employed, was a stairway of high steps that climbed up out of sight? Again, being very honest, what's demotivating about such a situation, assuming you want to stay and to do your best?

_____

_____

_____

_____

_____

The bad news is that as Brian sits in his car, he's feeling as low as the underground lot where his car is parked. But good news is coming.

Many years ago a man named Joseph stood in front of his brothers who had sold him into slavery. Now the tables were turned, and they stood before each other with their situations reversed. Joseph was second in command of all of Egypt, the same land he had come into as a slave. But now his brothers stood before him at his mercy and in grave need of his help.

Keeping that story of Joseph in mind, think back to Brian. While he couldn't have imagined it at the time, what if the tables were to turn some day? What if things actually changed so much that Brian became "The Bulldog's" boss! From a *worldly* perspective, how would you expect Brian to act toward his former tormentor?

_____

_____

_____

Let's go back now to Joseph with his brothers standing before him. That's a situation where the tables were turned if ever there was one. Only let's look at the way a godly person deals with their reversed situation: "As for you, you meant evil against me, but God meant it for good" (Genesis 50:20).

While we'll save a closer look at Joseph for another chapter, it's clear that Joseph wasn't looking for payback because he realized that God was in the process, even when things were tough. When life was unfair and any hope of change looked hopeless, Joseph never stopped factoring in a loving, living God. That's my challenge to you as well as you get ready to turn your perspective from where you've been to where you can go with small steps. Even if the problems you're seeking to move past or the areas of change you need to make are directly linked to a "bulldog," don't think that difficult person is the only person in the picture. Even when Joseph was in prison, Almighty God was with him; and while his own "bulldogs" meant what they did for evil, God turned it to good.

How can it help in dealing with a "bulldog" to know that even today God is and will turn the trials in your life into good?

_____

_____

_____

_____

two rays of light on a very dark day

There is a children's book titled *Alexander and the Terrible, Horrible, No Good, Very Bad Day*. On a day that could have been titled "Brian and the terrible, horrible, no good, very bad day," two positive things happened. Two different people in two different ways and in different places tag-teamed Brian—not in a negative way in piling on more discouragement but each bringing their own ray of hope on that very bad day, each one echoing the others heartfelt message without ever knowing or meeting or corresponding in advance. I think with Brian it was the incredible unlikelihood that something like that could happen that really opened his eyes to what was being shared, beginning with Andy's e-mail to his father.

Andy's E-mail

Take a moment if it's been a while, and go back to chapter 5. Read again Andy's e-mail to his father. While it may have been purposefully short of details about what they were doing on their missions, something came across crystal clear that was motivating Andy and his whole company of marines. It was the challenge to focus on one-inch changes. While "one inch" is an even smaller metaphor than the several "small steps" Eric then shared with Brian later that afternoon, take a moment to unpack this first "word picture" of change. What is there about one-inch changes that you think might have been so motivating to these marines in a situation where there were so much fluidity and so many challenging, unpredictable

2°

tasks before them? Why do you think "one inch" helped focus, encourage, and motivate them so much?

_____

_____

_____

_____

_____

Did you notice how, at the end of Andy's letter, Brian felt like he always received more encouragement out of letters from his son than he'd tried to put in his own letters to his son? Have you personally experienced that in corresponding or talking with people in difficult situations? Perhaps you've visited someone in the hospital where you've gone into their room with the idea of trying to cheer them up and found *them* encouraging you. For many of us who support and pray for God's protection and his best for our men and women overseas, if you write some of them, you'll find the same thing to be true. In trying to encourage them in a terribly difficult situation, their words often bring far more encouragement back to those of us safe and sound in our own beds. (And if you don't have a specific serviceman or woman in mind to write, I suggest going to www.anysoldier.com or www.lettersfromhomeprogram.org. Either site can help you link a letter to a member of our armed forces deployed in harm's way who would appreciate knowing of your prayers and support for their service to our country.)

In addition, if you have older children, have they ever surprised you with encouraging words or unexpected but timely, helpful advice? In this case Andy does both. It's he who lifts up his father while he's in a difficult situation. What is it, do you think, about our kids or those in challenging situations that can at times make them the best dispensers of the "heart" medicine we need?

_____

_____

Eric's Meeting with Brian

When Brian and Eric met at a local coffee shop, a great deal took place in a short period of time. Without recounting the entire meeting, which you can interact about with your small group if you like, I'd like to pick out several things to reflect on, journal on, and discuss if you're in a small group.

The first thing was early in these two men's conversation when Eric shared that he knew Brian and Jennie were struggling. If you remember, that shocked Brian. He thought his subtle hints hadn't given away much of the problems he faced at home. Eric, however, saw right through his vague comments and shared how his own marriage had been in trouble and this *2 Degree Difference* concept had made a real difference for them.

How do you explain Brian's surprise that his friend had seen through his veiled references that he and his wife were having trouble? In line with this question, why do you think people feel that they can hide so much from others to whom their real situation is so obvious?

_____

_____

_____

_____

Looking at this from Eric's position, what do you think made this former soldier so sensitive to the few cues Brian had given? (One note: As you reflect on this, it might help to keep in mind a Shakespearean quote, "He laughs at scars who himself never bore a wound.")

2°

_____

_____

_____

_____

Spiritual Lights Coming On

When Eric used the same words that Brian had so recently read in his son's e-mail, _"one inch,"_ it really got Brian's attention. Can you think of a time when you became convinced that something wasn't just coincidence but you were part of something where God's hand was directing, combining, or leading events?

_____

_____

_____

_____

_____

In addition to answering that question, how easy or difficult has it been for you to see or to feel strongly that there is some kind of divine design behind the seeming coincidences in your life? For example, initially it was difficult for Brian to see or at least consciously admit there was any type of God connection to the e-mail and Eric's comments. While Brian was a committed Christian, he did not come from a tradition that commonly attributed everyday decisions or "coincidental" actions to God's hand. However, as the conversation continued that day, even very conservative Brian felt more and more that the e-mail and coffee time were indeed a divine appointment. That was Brian's thinking process in part.

In your group or in the journal space below, what are your thoughts and background regarding God's intervention in our everyday affairs?

_____

_____

_____

_____

_____

As Brian looked back, he became more and more convinced that what happened at that coffee shop that day was a "line in the sand" time in his life. And remember, the first decision he made was simply to stay and hear Eric out.

For many people there is a decision *before* the decision. For example, C. S. Lewis, in coming to faith, wrote that the key turning point for him was moving from being an atheist to *a theist*. That was the toughest decision. From theist to Christ was a much smaller step for Lewis than the first.

Let's turn to your life story and when you first read the *2 Degree Difference* or were walked through the idea behind it by a friend or teacher. Was there a decision *before* the decision for you? In other words, was there a predecision that set up your willingness to look closely at this concept or even start to live it out?

_____

_____

_____

_____

_____

In your journaling and personal discussions, you've now looked at your past—and perhaps at what held you back in the past—taken a close look at several life areas where there might be gaps that could use 2 Degree

2°

changes (like the workplace, marriage, health, etc.), and now talked about the decision-making process you made that has brought you to this point. It's time to turn our focus to Eric's argument on why the *2 Degree Difference* can be so powerful and from there to look at specific areas in your life where this concept could be applied.

could there really be something to a life of inches and degrees?

If you've ever watched or been to a major automobile race like the Indianapolis 500 or a major NASCAR race, you know that a pace car launches in front of the race cars on the track. When everyone in the pack is motoring at a steady speed and lined and ready to race, the pace car pulls off, and the real race begins. That's where we are in the book and in this journaling process. We've finished with the "prelims" and it's time to hit the pedal! We'll do that as we look quickly at the five major arguments Eric makes in support of the *2 Degree Difference* found in this journal chapter and the next.

Eric made a drawing on a sheet of paper to help Brian see his key points. You'll see that diagram reproduced here in the journal. Let's start then with Eric's first drawing and the first supporting point he makes that small changes can change everything.

Positive Change Starts with Fixing Broken Windows

In the *2 Degree Difference*, Eric makes the case for doing small things, even when facing big problems, by illustrating the "broken-window theory" of crime prevention. Eric shared examples that Brian had seen in his travels of a crime-ridden New York City. He also shared the tremendous success that Mayor Giuliani found in focusing on small things, like fixing broken windows. Eric illustrated how the murder rate went down from over 2,400 to 642 in his last year in office. Giuliani and his team also stopped the "squeegee men" problem and in the process erased more than five thousand felonies a week (*Leadership* by Rudolph Giuliani). But listen to a Giuliani quote that makes an incredibly important point: "We attacked crime immediately, but we knew that it would take time to show results. And reducing the number of crimes wouldn't be enough; people had to see an improvement, not just hear about it. If crime went down but the existing amount of pushing and shoving, urinating on the streets, and other quality-of-life issues remained the same, we would never have a convincing case that life was better. We had to get people to feel safe."[1]

Here then is one of the reasons small changes, 2 Degree changes, are so incredibly powerful. Many times, in many different situations, people quit a commitment because it takes too long for them to see any results. There may be good things going on underneath the surface or behind the scenes, but Giuliani knew that for change to really take root, "people had to see an improvement, not just hear about it."

Think about the last diet you were on. (If you've never been on a diet, then talk to a friend about whether the following is true.) Most people fail at losing weight because the changes they make are so big and dramatic and it takes so long to see any real results that they simply give up. Giuliani knew that there is something incredibly self-reinforcing about quickly seeing tangible results.

This idea of doing something small but also visual and tangible led the mayor's team to pick on the graffiti problem in the subways. One of the first things a visitor to New York does is ride the subways. Unfortunately, at that time it also meant that the first thing a visitor to New York saw was every single subway car filled inside and out with spray-painted gang signs, scrawl, and profanity.

Believe it or not, this was a perfect problem for them to tackle using the "broken window theory." Giuliani made the decision that anyone caught spraying on graffiti would be arrested and fingerprinted. (They were left alone before because the police were concentrating on bigger crimes. Now these small crimes were given a zero tolerance.) Also, the decision was made that no subway car on any train could leave the station in the morning if it had graffiti painted on it. They started with one subway line, then the next, and each night crew worked sometimes all night to paint and repaint the cars. People quickly began to see a different New York. And amazingly, when things *looked* better, people began to act better.

Write here or discuss: Have you ever given up on a diet or on some other big commitment like reading through the Bible every day for a year because you didn't see results quickly enough in lost weight or increased knowledge or motivation to read God's Word? Share an example where a lack of positive feedback stopped an attempt you made to change.

_____

_____

_____

_____

_____

Imagine a house on your street that sits vacant with a number of broken windows. Then one day, even though you don't know who is doing it or why, the windows are fixed, and bright clean glass gleams as you walk by each day. Then it gets a boost of paint. Then the weeds are removed. How would seeing these changes encourage you?

_____

_____

_____

_____

Think about an area in your life where you'd like to apply the *2 Degree Difference*—diet, spending control, finishing chores, or being closer to a child or spouse, for example. Think about doing a great deal and seeing no change for a long period of time or doing a little and seeing a little change consistently. Do you buy in to the thought that *seeing* small changes more quickly reinforces a feeling that things can change? Why or why not?

_____

_____

_____

_____

One last thought: In an upcoming chapter we'll talk about Brian's continuing to do small things for his wife month after month with no apparent movement in their relationship. Why didn't he give up? Before you answer, think about this question: Is it reinforcing enough if we see we've done something small, even if we don't see long-term or great results quickly?

_____

_____

_____

_____

"Broken windows" is the first drawing Eric made. Here's the second.

Change and a One-Inch Frame

The second drawing Eric made was of a one-inch picture frame. That's a small frame and hard to find if you actually go looking for one. Eric had found one and set it on the table to illustrate this next aspect of the *2 Degree Difference* to Brian. Eric based what he shared in this box on the book *Bird by Bird* by Anne Lamott, and particularly on her story about her brother. Her brother faced a huge challenge: to write a term paper on fifty-two birds of North America overnight—an assignment that had been made three months before. The prospect was overwhelming. The solution was either to give up or to succeed by writing about them "bird by bird."

Anne Lamott quotes the famous novelist E. L. Doctorow as saying, "Writing a novel is like driving a car at night. You can only see as far as your headlights, but you can make the whole trip that way."[2] That's another way of saying, "Write just enough to fill a one-inch frame." Here again, stop to write in your journal and/or discuss just why this act of writing a little can help you finish the biggest writing task.

———————————————————————————————

———————————————————————————————

———————————————————————————————

———————————————————————————————

———————————————————————————————

Can you see yourself writing an entire novel? Writing a long book is hard, arduous work. But it's nearly impossible to "write the whole thing." It's challenging but doable if you write it "inch by inch."

You've looked at "fixing broken windows" in fighting out-of-control crime and writing a whole novel just by filling in a "one-inch frame." Both are ways of doing small things that give people, and ourselves, a picture that we're moving, even if it is just one inch at a time.

Let's look now at the third argument Eric offers for making 2 Degree changes. At the end of chapter 6, in spite of himself, Brian is starting to feel some hope. He's been so discouraged in the past. What do you think is going on inside Brian's head in hearing about broken windows and one-inch frames?

———————————————————————————————

_____

_____

_____

_____

We're finished with our reflection on the first two points Eric made. Now it's time for those frustrated directors among us to get ready to make that square!

Notes

1. Rudolph W. Giuliani with Ken Kurson, *Leadership* (New York: Miramax Books, 2002), 41.

2. Anne Lamott, *Bird by Bird* (New York: Anchor Book/DoubleDay, 1994).

a very different case for change piles up

Eric drew two more images on his "show and tell" paper. Each provided another "outside the box" example of small steps that you can take to make a big difference in your life. In this journal chapter, we'll highlight how a small change can not only open up your eyes and perspective but it can also keep your life moving in a positive direction. Eric continued to build his case for small changes using a director's square and a steering wheel.

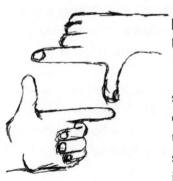

Focusing on Small Things Helps Us See Unnoticed Things

When Eric had Brian make a director's square and frame a small area at the far end of the coffee shop, Brian actually saw more than he was aware was there. The idea of shrinking our focus so that we can see more is something we've seen photographers and directors do in framing a shot. It also gives us another "outside the box" way of understanding how a 2 Degree focus can change our view of life and change. And if that seems paradoxical or confusing, it's something millions of Americans are drawn to each week.

SEEING LESS CAN CHANGE EVERYTHING

While Eric focused on a movie-making analogy to illustrate this point about small changes to Brian, this same principle of seeing more by focusing on less is all around us. For example, if you're like many millions of Americans, you've seen this perspective catch some of the worst criminals of our day. If you've ever watched *Cold Case Files*, or any of the many spin-off shows or movies like it, then you've seen how viewing things through a "director's square" focus can explode your understanding of large, even unseen things.

While a detective may grapple to get the big picture of a crime, the crime scene investigators, lab technicians, and forensic experts shrink their perspective to do their job. To surface something that will break open the case, they start by breaking down a large crime area into small frames. They look at small things, sometimes smaller than the eye can see; and in so doing, they can sometimes see more of what actually happened during the crime. Frankly, if I were a crook, I'd be scared to death with all the tools and techniques now being employed against bad people. Most of us have seen how the direction of that one blood splatter, or the presence of that one tiny hair or partial fingerprint, or that single out-of-place blade of grass, or that unexpected shred of fiber leads to a breakthrough in a case that had gone cold. And of course there is the ultimate narrowing of a DNA sample that can exclude or technically narrow out billions of others on the planet so that a prosecutor can point the finger at that one guilty person.

Small things count at a crime scene. More than one hundred years ago people devoured Sherlock Holmes stories. That's because the world's greatest detective back then used tiny clues to solve unsolvable crimes. We see that every night on television as small things open up a new lead or change the entire course of an investigation.

Granted, that's kind of a creepy way of understanding this aspect of small things—powerful—but creepy. So to get back to a more positive focus, let's go back to Eric's director's square.

When you read about those grown men at the coffee shop making "squares," did you stop to do it yourself? If not, here's the perfect time and chance for you to write down and share your thoughts on the process—and for your whole small group to do this if you're working through the journal with others.

Look across a long room or at a landscape and make that "square." What *more* can you see by seeing less?

_____

_____

_____

_____

_____

Let's apply this idea of narrowing our focus to see how it can positively impact our spiritual life, actually opening up for us a deeper, stronger faith by narrowing our focus. For while you may not have seen it before, this director's square idea is woven throughout the Scriptures.

For example, there's the familiar passage in Psalm 90:12: "Teach us to number our days, that we may present to You a heart of wisdom."

Keeping in mind all we've talked about so far about narrowing our focus, why do you think that being able to present a "heart of wisdom" to God is linked with "numbering our days"? How are numbering days and wisdom related?

_____

_____

_____

_____

_____

As you've thought through the question above, have you ever felt or said, "That day just got away from me!" If so, that's another way to understand the psalmist's counsel. We're often so busy just getting by that we set our focus on the weekend, or the next day off, or the next holiday. In the process the days in between escape us. In short, we can see more of what God has for us when we narrow our focus to *this* day, to that single person we're talking with, or to that specific task we're on. Jesus teaches us, "Give us this day our daily bread" (Matthew 6:11).

Here's another way of seeing how narrowing our focus can help us see more of who God is and what he does. It's also something that explains why the Lord is so insistent in his Word that we attend church.

WHEN GOD'S PRESENCE FILLS A PLACE

Have you ever been at church and sung a song or had a worship leader ask Jesus to "fill this place" with his presence? Technically and theologically that's redundant and unnecessary to ask or sing. It's not like Jesus has been off somewhere else, and now we're asking him somehow to come back into the picture. Rather, it's a poetic way of asking that *our* focus be narrowed so that in this place, at this time we can experience Jesus more fully. To explain this, let's look at the world's greatest "grand opening."

There was a time in the Old Testament when Almighty God gathered an entire nation to one place at one time. He narrowed those people's focus to a single place, and in so doing, he taught them more about his grandeur and majesty. Here's how it happened.

In 2 Chronicles 5, you'll find history's greatest "grand opening." The largest group to celebrate a "grand opening" wasn't the thousands who showed up at the Hard Rock Café in London where lines of people stretched for almost a mile to get a glimpse of some celebrities. Almighty God gathered hundreds of thousands, an entire nation, to one place at one time. Just on the main stage itself were thousands of singers; cymbal, harp, and lyre players; and even 120 trumpets announcing the opening of the temple in Jerusalem.

If you've ever been a part of a start-up church, you know what it's like finally to have a place of your own. Instead of having to set out signs, then set up the stage and sound system at the grade school where you're meeting, then take down everything at the grade school, and then take down all the signs, at long last God's people had a place of their own to worship.

On that incredible day of celebration, "Then the house, the house of the LORD, was filled with a cloud, so that the priests could not stand to minister because of the cloud, for the glory of the LORD filled the house of God" (2 Chronicles 5:13–14).

"Now when Solomon had finished praying, fire came down from heaven and consumed the burnt offering and the sacrifices, and the glory of the LORD filled the house" (2 Chronicles 7:1).

It was an incredible day as the God of the universe, wrapped in clouds and with literal "fireworks" falling from the sky, let his people know that they now had a place where they could come and worship him.

Here's the question: Did God in any way limit who he was by narrowing the people's focus to that temple in order to worship him? Explain your answer below and, if you're with a small group, discuss your thoughts as well.

_____

_____

_____

_____

I wish I were a church historian, or better yet, a Ph.D. in church architecture throughout the ages. For then I could do a far better job of explaining why people coming into a place of worship are often moved to gain a greater view of a limitless God. You'd think that the last thing the God of the universe would want is for people to come inside a building, even if it's a beautiful temple or a great cathedral or even one of today's modern church building marvels. Why didn't the Lord just leave his people to sit on a riverbank, up on a mesa, or outside in a clearing to worship him? Isn't more, *more*? Or by narrowing our focus to the inside of a cathedral or even to the inside of a high school gym, does something actually happen when we shrink our perspective, that draws us to think and see more clearly a God who made all the stars and stretched out the heavens?

Most likely you aren't a church historian or church architect either. (And if you are, then please lead this discussion with your group and mail or e-mail us your thoughts so we can communicate this more effectively!) But just from your experience as an everyday person like the rest of us, think about walking inside a church or cathedral. See if you can capture on paper and in words with your small group what happens when we meet inside, to worship the God of the heavens.

_____

_____

_____

_____

Eric shared with Brian a physical way of narrowing our perspective, which can actually be extremely powerful in allowing us to see more. We've also looked at two biblical examples of how seeing less helps us to see more. (And we didn't even mention why "inductive Bible study" can be so life changing. *Inductive* means taking a single verse and looking at every word. As you study a verse closely—look at each definition, tense, person, and word placement—you start seeing more and more by narrowing your focus as well. If you do, you'll often find God's Word reading *you* instead of you reading it!)

Let's look now at the fourth picture Eric gave Brian of the power of small things. This one shows us the ability of small changes to keep our life on track.

Quit Making 2 Degree Changes and You're Headed for a Wreck

The last image Eric drew to show the importance of small things was a steering wheel. This picture is much easier for most of us to grasp because we're so used to getting in a car and grabbing hold of a steering wheel and making 2 Degree changes—lots of them, if we're committed to being a safe driver and staying between the lines. As Eric shared with Brian, head down the road making constant 10 or 20 degree turns of the wheel, and you're heading to jail or at least for a session of hopping on one foot in a sobriety test. But small, consistent changes of the wheel keep us heading safely in the direction we want to go and out of the big trouble that comes from straying outside the lines.

Let's try to illustrate Eric's "steering wheel" concept by picking a business example. Did you know that failing to understand the importance of small things will lead to 93 percent of small businesses that are launched, going out of business in three years or less? That's a 93-percent failure rate of people's dreams and goals and only a 7-percent likelihood that you'll still be doing faux painting, or making pizzas, or doing computer maintenance for longer than thirty-six months if you start your own business. Why do so many small businesses fail, and why do those who are a part of the 7 percent last?

In study after study, book after book, it's the small things (as you might have imagined). For example, let's take a person who makes outstanding chili. He enters every chili contest in a four-state area and consistently comes home with the blue ribbon (while sending the judges home with heartburn). His friends love his twelve-alarm chili. Total strangers start knocking on his door to ask if it's chili day. Time and again he hears, "You ought to start your own chili restaurant. Your chili is so good!" And so at a transition point in his regular day-job life, he quits and starts the 3-D House of Chili. The place fills up with people. More people and more money, and soon there's another 3-D House of Chili and then a third. And then everyone lives happily ever after, right? Actually, 93 percent of the time all three chili houses will be gone in three years, even with a passionate person with an outstanding product and great optimism that failure would never happen to them.

Why such a drastic drop-out rate?

There's a huge difference between making great chili and running a chili restaurant. The person winning all the ribbons is good at making chili for a few people. He's probably an outstanding cook in his own kitchen. But now he's not just a cook for a few. He has to learn to cook for a lot of people. Then he also has to learn to train other cooks to be as good and passionate as he is. And because it's a small business, he has to become a top-notch marketer, and he's the bookkeeper and the customer care specialist and the financier to work with the bank and the maintenance person and the janitor and the cleanup crew. He's not making chili anymore;

he's running a chili business. And if he doesn't narrow his focus—or as the best-selling book, *The "E" Myth: Why Most Small Businesses Don't Work and What to Do About It* explains—if he doesn't "manualize" everything he does, he's headed for the 93-percent failure pile.

Take the way McDonalds makes French fries. Very few McDonalds ever fail. That's because every McDonalds follows a manual that breaks down the "McDonalds way of doing things" into small, understandable steps, like what to do to make the perfect McDonald's fry. They break things down into small steps and procedures so that whether you go into a McDonalds in London, England, or Paris, Texas, every fry looks and smells and tastes the same. And it's broken down into small enough steps that even a high-school student can master what it takes to make people want to "jumbo-size" their meal with an extra large order of fries.

Most small businesses never get to the place where they chart their business in a manual of the small things it takes to succeed. As a result, they quit doing the small things that made them successful in the first place: the attention to small detail in the sauce, the small things they did or said when people first came in, the small ways they served their chili to the judges so that it was hot and its flavor was at its peak. Instead, we get busy, things grow, we're doing more and more, and then more and more still, and finally our quality goes down and our business goes under. Ask an executive at a company that's growing 40 percent a year how difficult his or her job is becoming. Big growth often ends in a company's failure because they quit doing the small things.

Don't worry. At the end of this book, you won't be asked to break your spiritual life or marriage into a series of six-inch manuals or walk around with your hands making a square everywhere you go! But small things are a key to seeing more and keeping us on track. To go back to the business example above, if you've ever worked at a restaurant, here's your chance to shine in this journaling or sharing section.

What were some small things you were trained to do when you worked at a restaurant? If you never worked at one, then why do you think in any business, attention to small things can keep or drive you out of business?

_____

_____

_____

_____

_____

Moving past the business example, let's take our first specific look at how small things can make a difference in other areas as well.

What is one small thing you can do to strengthen a friendship you have and keep it on track? Note your answer below.

_____

_____

_____

_____

In your health, what is just one small thing you can do to increase your likelihood of not catching a cold this cold season?

_____

_____

_____

_____

At your job—or if you're a student, at school—what is just one small thing you can do to help you keep on track of a project or complete an assignment?

_____

_____

_____

_____

We'll go much deeper into each of these areas, but hopefully Eric's case for change involving small things is piling up a compelling argument for you to being making 2 Degree changes as well. When I teach the *2 Degree Difference* at seminars and in classes, I literally bring a steering wheel with me. People get the picture almost instantly when I hold it up. To have a successful company or relationship, you simply must make small, consistent course corrections if you're going to arrive at your destination safely.

You've seen and reflected on these four images and arguments for doing small things to change everything. We've got one more to come that indeed acts to pull all that's been shared together. However, just before we move forward, of the four pictures Eric drew (broken window, picture frame, director's square, steering wheel), which one do you think is the strongest argument for making 2 Degree changes? Why?

_____

_____

_____

_____

Which of his four pictures do you find *least* persuasive or understandable?

_____

_____

_____

_____

Let's move now to that fifth picture he drew that should be of great interest to each of us.

a great secret that grabbed hold of brian's life

2°

Eric shared one last thing with Brian that day in the coffee shop. It was a drawing that looked like a dollar bill placed in the center of the page. It was meant to pull all the drawings together.

2°

Good and Evil Grow at Compound Interest

Eric set up his last example by asking Brian if there were someone in his life whom he was having a struggle with. That's a question I'd like to put to you as well as we continue our journal reflections. You don't have to put down this person's name, but please do come up with one person either in the present or recent past who has been a challenge to like—and challenge may be an understatement. With that person in mind, let's look again at C. S. Lewis's quote and Brian's commentary.

> "The worldly man treats certain people kindly because he 'likes' them."

Eric read this sentence with particular emphasis on the word *likes*.

> "The Christian, trying to treat everyone kindly, finds himself liking more and more people as he goes on—including people he could not have imagined himself liking at the beginning." Emphasis this time was placed on the word *imagined*.

If you're serious about the Christian faith, you'll notice there are often uncomfortable statements, like "love your enemies" or "do good to those who despise you." What Lewis points out not only goes against our grain when it comes to someone we don't like; it also points out something that seems like a jump from A to C. It just doesn't seem possible. But Lewis points out that for the Christian, there is a gradual movement away from dislike and even toward liking even unlikable people, even our enemies. And if that seems impossible to you right now, as it certainly did for Brian the day he'd gotten his probation letter, then know that it's truth not fiction. And please take the time to read and discuss the following story that highlights that truth.

A Christmas Day like No Other

Lieutenant John McCain was on a bombing run over Hanoi in early 1967. Just as the Navy A-4 fighter-bomber he piloted released its bomb load, a surface-to-air missile blew off the right wing of his plane. McCain remembers pulling the ejection cable but little else of those first few moments. Witnesses said his chute had barely opened before he smashed into a body of shallow water.

McCain had landed in the middle of Truc Bach Lake.

In the middle of the city of Hanoi. In the middle of the day.

There would be no escape. McCain was dragged out of the lake, his body screaming from the pain of a shattered right leg and a broken right shoulder—broken after the first soldier to reach him smashed his rifle butt into it. He was initially denied medical attention until his captors discovered that they had in their hands the son of an Admiral of the United States Navy. Neither McCain nor his captors knew it at the time, but his father was soon to be promoted to CINPAC, Commander of all American forces in the Pacific.

Lieutenant McCain was taken to the infamous prison for captured flyers his captors called The Plantation and the Americans called, tongue in cheek, The Hanoi Hilton. This place of torture, beatings, deprivation, intimidation, and hatred would be his home from 1967 until 1973.

Of course McCain could have gone home after only one year.

He was called in one day to face the notorious camp commander and was actually given the chance to go home. He could be released the next day! But McCain found out that it would mean he would jump ahead of five other officers who had been in prison longer than he had. It would mean he would be free, but it would also mean he had to break the code of the camp that kept the men's morale together: "First in, first out." Meaning, the one who had been there the longest should be the first one to go home. McCain would have been free, but he knew that they would have used his release as a psychological tool against the others day after day. So he said no to being released ahead of the others; and so the beatings, harassment, and torture continued. Even one day close to Christmas.

In his book *Faith of My Fathers*, McCain tells how one interrogator particularly delighted in brutality. He would approach McCain each day and demand that he bow before him. If McCain refused or even if he did bow, the guard would smash his fist into the side of his head, knocking him to the ground. In McCain's words, "Those encounters were not episodic. They occurred every morning for nearly two years."[1]

2°

It was now a few days before Christmas, and McCain endured one of the worst beatings he'd ever been given. He had been forced to attend yet another interrogation session. He was tied to a chair and beaten senseless. McCain awoke, all by himself, lying on his side, still tied to his chair where they had left him in the room. There were always gun guards at the door. Usually there were soldiers who had been wounded so badly in battle that they couldn't be shipped to the front lines. There was a gun guard at the door that night when McCain awoke.

The two men's eyes met and quickly, the young guard walked over to him. It was forbidden for guards to make any contact with the prisoners if an officer wasn't present. However, silently, without once looking directly at McCain, the guard loosened the ropes that bound him and left him alone in the room. Incredible relief flowed over McCain as blood flowed back into stiff, aching limbs. The gun guard's night shift usually lasted from 10:00 p.m. until 4:00 a.m. Just before his shift ended, the same guard returned and tightened McCain's ropes.

Had that guard been caught helping McCain, he would have immediately been shot. But why did he do it? McCain would find out on Christmas Day.

On Christmas Day, a few days later, the prisoners were treated to a better than usual dinner, including the privilege of standing outside their cells for five minutes. They could exercise or stretch or just stand outside and look at the trees and sky. As they stood outside their prison doors, the same gun guard who had risked his life to loosen McCain's ropes approached him. Here's what McCain writes about the encounter: "He walked up and stood silently next to me. Again, he didn't smile or look at me. He just stared at the ground in front of us. After a few moments had passed he rather nonchalantly used his sandaled foot to draw a cross in the dirt. We both stood wordlessly looking at the cross until, after a minute or two, he rubbed it out and walked away."

Where does a person get the strength to help someone, even an enemy guard helping their prisoner? If the cross can bring two mortal enemies together, then it can bring us closer together with those we struggle to like. Even, as Lewis said, with people we couldn't imagine ever liking.

Having read that story, what are your thoughts about the way these two men, the prisoner and the guard, would have looked at each other and at life differently? Today Senator John McCain says he carries no hatred for his captors of nearly seven years. Do you think this incident might have had something to do with the reason that is so? Take some time to reflect back on this story and what it says about the anger we carry toward others.

_____

_____

_____

_____

_____

_____

Remember, we're still focusing on people who are hard to like, or as Lewis said, people we "couldn't imagine" liking. Here's the extended quote from Lewis that was where Eric came up with the image of the dollar bill to lie across all the other pictures. Take some time to review this key insight into small, 2 Degree changes:

> The Christian, trying to treat every one kindly, finds himself liking more and more people as he goes on—including people he could not have imagined himself liking at the beginning. The rule then for all of us is perfectly simple. Do not waste time bothering whether you "love" your neighbor, act as if you do. And soon as we do this we find one of the great secrets. When you are behaving as if you love someone, you will presently come to love him. If you injure someone you dislike, you will find yourself disliking him more. If you do him a good turn, you will find yourself disliking him less.
>
> This is because good and evil both increase at compound interest.
>
> And that is why the little decisions you and I make every day are of such infinite importance. The smallest good act today is the capture of a strategic point from which, a few months later, you may be able to go on to victories you never dreamed of. An apparently trivial

indulgence in lust or anger today is the loss of a ridge or railway line or bridgehead from which the enemy may launch an attack otherwise impossible.[2]

There's so much here to discuss. First, do you think that Lewis uses the phrase "one of the great secrets" loosely or as an exaggeration? Explain your answer.

_____

_____

_____

This is also where Lewis links small acts of "good or evil" as growing at "compound interest." Before looking at what Lewis meant by that, let's take a closer look at what *compound interest* means.

Business 101 and Compound Interest

If you're a business student, when you're taught about compound interest, you learn that a sum invested is paid when due, and then interest is paid again at a fixed point on the new total of principal and interest. And so principal and interest grow until in time more interest is being paid on the interest accrued than the initial investment of principal! Put another way, compound interest (technically Compound Annual Growth Rate [CAGR]) can be formulated using this formula:

$$CAGR + (FV/PV)1/n—1$$

Here FV is the future value, PV the present value, and n is the number of years.

For example, let's say in twenty years you want to have $10,000 in a bank account. Let's also say that you know you have a locked-in interest rate of 5 percent that compounds each year. Using a CAGR calculator you can find on many Web sites like www.moneychimp.com, you can see what will happen if you put $3,769 into a savings account today and just leave the money in that account where it will compound annually at 5 percent. In twenty years you'll have your $10,000. That's a good amount of growth! But watch this.

Let's say you received an inheritance of $40,000. Go ahead and spend $2,310 on a big screen DVD TV. But put the remaining $37,690 in the bank just as you did above. Put $37,690 in the bank at 5 percent interest for twenty years and never take it out. Let it grow at compound interest. Then go back to the bank after twenty years and one day, and you'll have $100,000 you can withdraw.

That's how banks and wealthy people get so wealthy over time. They put large sums (like $37,690) in the bank and forget about it for twenty years and wake up with thousands of dollars.

With that in mind, let's go back to Lewis's analogy.

"Good and evil grow at compound interest."

For journaling and discussion: Do you agree with Lewis? If not, why? If so, why? Can you think of a time in your life when small acts resulted in larger gain? If you're familiar with Lewis's writing, can you think of other times or ways he stated this truth?

_____

_____

_____

_____

_____

At this point in Brian's story, you read for the first time what we chose as the subtitle of *The 2 Two Degree Difference, "How Little Things Can Change Everything."* Small acts for Lewis were pictured as incredible growth generators for both good and evil. It's our prayer that as we move now into area after area of life, you'll be motivated to make small "good" investments into your health, home, and heart for God. Just a few more questions before we move from "theory" to practice.

Eric left Brian with those five pictures and with a promise that he'd back them up the next time they met with specific Scriptures that showed the same benefits of making small changes. I've already given you a number of solid biblical reasons and examples where more isn't more and where being faithful in a little is a key to gaining much. But for Brian there was a battle before the battle. He was sitting in the coffee shop, confident already that this 2 Degree change idea had merit, but then came those doubts.

For you, personally, how certain are you that small changes can indeed change everything? That small steps can help you in your health? Strengthen your home? Build stronger friendships? Help you break bad habits? Turn around a struggling marriage or difficult relationship with a child? Just answer that question of certainty here.

_____

_____

_____

_____

If you are certain, or if you need more convincing, what thoughts, words, memories, or specific doubts spring up in your mind at this half-way point in the journal that change can really happen in your life, even if you do small things?

_____

_____

_____

_____

Brian came out of that coffee shop determined, committed to try this 2 Degree change concept in at least one area of his life. That's all I'm asking of you at this halfway point, to pick one area out of the several we'll go through in the remaining chapters and commit to making a few small steps, 2 Degree changes.

If you're willing to do that, then sign and date the box below. Let it be a contract with yourself that you're at least going to give the *2 Degree Difference* an opportunity to bear interest in your life. Commit that once you've worked through this journal and picked and written down a few small steps you're going to try in just one area, that you'll in fact live out those small changes. While you may not know everything about "broken-window theory" or "director's squares" or "compound interest," you can base your decision below on the fact that Almighty God has said that he can take a little and turn it into a lot.

Notes

1. John McCain, *Faith of My Fathers* (New York: Random House, 1999), 228.

2. C. S. Lewis, *Mere Christianity*, 21.

I, _____,
having come this far in reading and journaling,
commit to picking one area after finishing this
book. I commit to living out a few small 2 Degree
changes and trust that they will indeed grow at
compound interest for the benefit of others, and
to be more of the person I feel God wants me to
become. As my Lord is my witness, on this _____
_____ day of _____, 20_____ .

_____
(Signature)

the 2 Degree Difference
challenges a daughter
whose heart is closed

As stated earlier in the book, "Brian made the commitment to give 2 Degree changes a try. But in his mind he picked an area that to him was so challenging he felt sure there was no way it would work. In picking his relationship with his teenage daughter as his launch point, he thought he could prove to himself, and to Eric, that this 'small stuff' idea wasn't as powerful as Eric was convinced it was. Sure, reducing the murder rate in New York City by 67 percent by doing small things was an incredible feat. But Brian knew he would never be a mayor and face those kinds of problems. The problems facing him, like reestablishing a relationship with his teenage daughter, were his world-class challenges."

For discussion or journaling: For many, challenges at home can seem more difficult than issues at work or with those outside one's family. Would you agree or disagree with this statement and why?

_____

_____

_____

_____

_____

_____

$2°$

In this journal chapter, let's focus on parents and, in particular, on how a parent can build or rebuild a relationship with a child by making 2 Degree changes. I'd like to recommend to you a parenting book, *Parenting from Your Strengths* (John Trent, Rodney Cox, and Eric Tooker, Broadman & Holman, 2006). It's a short, fun read that is filled with great ideas for parents to understand their strengths and those of their child. It also highlights the discussion you'll find in the next chapter on marriage. Here in this chapter let's look at the great task of parenting, and how 2 Degree changes can help make a great difference.

After a number of pages of journaling, please read this next teaching section and ask yourself, *Did I get my parents' blessing?*

2 Degree Ways to Connect with and Bless Your Child

It's hinted at in this chapter that in earlier years Brian had worked hard at building a good relationship with his daughter. That was true. While things with Amy now that she was in junior high had become very much at arm's length, that wasn't always the case. When Amy was younger, Brian had done several things that would pave the way for his 2 Degree changes to take hold so quickly. Regardless of whether you've done these in the past, it's never too late to begin. And as you go through these small-step suggestions, you'll see a "Personal Reflection" question at the end of each. Honestly evaluate whether you personally received any of these small things from your own parents growing up.

FOUR SMALL THINGS TO MAKE SURE YOUR CHILD HAS YOUR BLESSING AND SOFTEN THE GROUND FOR 2 DEGREE CHANGE

In the Old Testament you see twins, Jacob and Esau, who fought over their father's blessing. Jacob received it and walked away from his father beaming. Esau missed it, and when he did, "He cried out with an exceedingly great and bitter cry, and said to his father, 'Bless me, even me also, O my father!'" (Genesis 27:34).

I have written extensively on this (see *The Blessing*, John Trent and Gary Smalley, Thomas Nelson Publishers, rev. 2004) and teach "the blessing" as a core relationship concept at The Center for StrongFamilies. It's a concept that highlights the incredibly deep need in each person's life for their own parent's blessing. What was it then that Jacob received from his father and Esau failed to receive? It's five small things that were always a part of the blessing given children, whether by a mother, father, or grandparent. And while it might be surprising to some, when you look at clinical studies of what makes a strong family today, you'll see these same five elements of the Old Testament blessing surface time and again.

First, practice small acts of appropriate touch.

From the moment of birth, children cry out for someone to be there for them. A newborn boy's tiny fingers and chubby arms reach out to be held. A tiny baby girl's mouth involuntarily sucks the air, searching for her mother. Quivering lips of both let out a precious cry for the lost warmth of the womb.

With all the trauma and exhaustion of traveling through the birth canal and into a brand-new world, babies who are wrapped up in a blanket and placed in a loving parent's arms often immediately fall asleep. Despite all the tactile and temperature changes, the bright lights, the unfamiliar sounds and smells, attachment overcomes anxiety. Having someone touch and hold them brings a deep sense of rest.

That is true of babies, and it continues to be true throughout a person's life. In the strongest of families, you find appropriate, meaningful touch when the children are younger and as they get older. As they get older of course, appropriate touch may be a handshake or a hug, holding their hand for a moment at church or in the car, ruffling their hair, or even wrestling with them on the floor when they're young.

How important are simple acts of touch? I grew up in a single-parent home. My father divorced my mother when my older brother was two and my twin brother and I were two months old. She never remarried, and she worked full-time to raise three rambunctious boys. However, while there were challenges galore, one thing was never missing from the shelf—appropriate, meaningful touch.

Every day from preschool through high school without exception my mother would drive us to school on her way to work, and when she stopped, we had to give her a hug.

2°

Hugging your mother when you get dropped off at kindergarten is one thing. But by first and second grade, it was becoming an increasingly embarrassing ritual at the drop-off circle at school each morning. By third grade, we had plea-bargained with my mother to stop the car *before* we got to school so that we could hug her. And year after year we made her drop us farther and farther away from school! By junior high it was a hug before we walked out the door to get into the car!

Where we hugged her was negotiable, but hugging my mother wasn't an option. Every day, day after day, month after month, and year after year, we "hated" having to get our short hug from Mom. But really we didn't.

I finally met my father late in high school for the first time. I tried hard to build a relationship with him. I never succeeded in going any deeper than the weather report, and there was never any appropriate, meaningful touch. The only time I remember holding my father's hand was at 3:42 one afternoon just before he died.

I thank the Lord for the appropriate, meaningful touch that was a part of my home, thanks to my mother. On the last day of my mother's life, I held her hand as well. Of course, that was the last time of a countless number of times. That touch said to me what her words couldn't on that last day of her life. My mother was alert but couldn't speak on that last day of her life. She didn't need to use words however. Her touch said she loved me. Holding my hand said she was proud of me, said it would be all right even with her gone. Her touch spoke a novel full of words without a single word being spoken that day.

My mom died very late at night, and when she passed away, she was holding both my hand and my older brother Joe's hand on the other side of her.

There is a hole in the heart of a child who does not get his parent's blessing. I've seen it in six year olds and those who are in their nineties. I've seen that hole destroy marriages and have people with outstanding, world-class success feel that they're nothing deep inside—like one professional baseball player who has won every award a player at his position could win, and yet his greatest regret is, "If I'd just done a little more, maybe my father would have been proud of me."

One small way to make sure that your child has your blessing is by choosing to provide them with appropriate, meaningful touch that can say without words how valuable they are to you.

Personal Reflection: Did you get this small part of the blessing from your parent(s)? Can you remember a specific time or place where an act of appropriate, meaningful touch by them meant a great deal to you? If you're in a small group, can you share that time with your group?

_____

_____

_____

_____

A second small way to give your child your blessing: spoken words that attach high value to your child.

Kids need to know, verbally and even in our written words to them, that we love and value them deeply. That one/two punch of their hearing verbally from you that you think they have great value and worth is like turning a light on that helps guide them towards a positive future.

I realize that it's not easy for some of us to put our feelings into words. But when we do, it can leave a memory for a child, a blessing in their life, that stays with them all their life. Like this letter from a father you might never guess would write such a letter, to his daughter. Imagine that you're the one who receives it:

> *Dearest Joanne,*
>
> *Those beautiful quaking aspens that you've seen in the forest as we have driven along have one purpose in life. I would like to tell you about them because they remind me a lot of Mommy and you kids and me.*
>
> *These aspens are born and grow just to protect the spruce tree when it's born. As the spruce tree grows bigger and bigger, the aspens gradually grow old and tired; and they even die after a while. But the spruce, which has had its tender self protected in its childhood, grows into one of the forest's most wonderful trees.*

Now think about Mommy and me as aspens standing there quaking ourselves in the winds that blow, catching the cold snows of life, bearing the hot rays of the sun, all to protect you from those things until you are strong enough and wise enough to do them yourself. We aren't quaking from fear but from the joy of being able to see your lives develop and grow into tall, straight men and women.

Just like the spruce, you have almost reached the point where you don't need us as much as you used to. Now you stand like the young spruce, a pretty, straight young thing whose head is beginning to peer above the protection of Mommy and Daddy's watchfulness. . . .

I am telling you all this because from now on a lot of what you eventually become—a lovely woman, a happy woman, and a brilliant, popular woman—depends on you.

You can't go through life being these things and at the same time frowning. You can't achieve these things and be grumpy. You have to grow so that your every deed and look reflect the glory that is now in your heart and soul.

Smile. Think right. Believe in God and his worldwide forest of men and women. It's up to you.

I love you,
Daddy

What a letter from a father to his daughter who was getting ready to head off to college. It was dated June 11, 1948. "I still cry every time I read it," Joanne said of this letter in a newspaper article written almost fifty years later about her memories of her father. "He was a master with words. He was a romantic."

Who was this "word master" and loving "romantic"?

Try none other than a political figure of the 1960s. His name was Barry Goldwater, and he ran unsuccessfully for president in 1964 after a long term in the United States Senate. He also loved his children very much and committed to putting those words of love and guidance and faith into words they could hear and read.

How about you? You don't have to write a letter like Barry Goldwater unless you're gifted in words. But trust me. Your kids don't need flowery words; they just need *your* words. Spoken out loud or written down and handed to them on a special occasion. They need to know verbally and preferably often that you love them and that you think they're God's gift to you of the highest value.

Personal Reflection: Did you grow up with these two elements of the blessing? Did you hear often (or ever) *verbally* or even in writing that you were loved and of great value to your parents? If you can remember a specific time when you received such words, write and share that time as well.

_____

_____

_____

_____

_____

A *third small way to give your children your blessing is to point them toward a positive future.*

There is a wonderful verse in Jeremiah that illustrates this fourth small thing you can do that helps a child know she has your blessing. It's found in Jeremiah 29:11. "'For I know the plans that I have for you,' declares the LORD, 'plans for welfare and not for calamity to give you a future and a hope.'"

Children are literalists when it comes to what their parents say about them. If you want to take your healthy, normal baby and turn him into someone who often feels all his life that he's not valuable—unless he learns how to reverse the curse as you did in journal chapter 1—then say things to him like this when he gets into school: "Don't take math! That's for the smart kids!" or, "Where do you get off thinking a fat mess like you is going to get a date?" Aim low for your child, and he'll hit that target every time. But telling a child that he has great strengths that God can use and especially that God has a special future for him can be tremendously empowering.

I know that from personal experience. My twin brother, Jeff, was always a tremendous student. He's a cancer doctor today and graduated from every school he attended at or near the top of his class. He graduated magna cum laude. Back in high school, it was time for our major senior-year term paper. Right on cue and like always, Jeff received an A on his report. I received a D. I was devastated. Sure, I hadn't followed the formatting the teacher wanted. And I'd run out of typewriter ribbon and had to handwrite the last page. But I thought it was well written, even without footnotes. I had lost that page of the instructions. As I sat at our old kitchen table, I'll never forget hanging my head as my mother looked over my paper. I knew she had already seen Jeff's paper and his A. I didn't think I would get an A, but I had worked hard, even if it wasn't up to form.

"John," my mother said, "look at me."

My mom always did a tremendous job of making us make eye contact with her when she wanted to communicate something important.

"You left out footnotes, and your spacing is wrong, and there's the handwritten part." I knew all that already as I once again hung my head.

"But look at me," she said and I raised my eyes. "You may have missed on the form of the paper, but you're a great writer. You use words so well. I wouldn't be surprised if you grew up and helped other people with your words some day."

Trust me. At that time in my life, none of my teachers were telling me I was a great writer or even an average writer, much less that I had any kind of future in writing or helping people with my words. But my mother saw something and said something about my future. And in large part it was her belief in me that helped light up that part of my future as something possible when the opportunity came, not an impossible dream that "stupid" me shouldn't even aim for.

Personal Reflection: Did you grow up with a mother and/or father who helped you see that you had a positive, God-honoring future ahead of you? If you did, how did that help you as you faced trials and opportunities in the future? If you didn't, can you see how that lack of a parent feeling you could succeed in the future has been challenging? If so, how?

The fourth small way to help children know they have your blessing is with genuine commitment.

Kids need to know that we'll be there for them. I'm thankful that I had a mom who was there, thick or thin. Several years ago now, my wife Cindy and I spoke at a physicians conference in Colorado. We had the privilege of meeting a couple about our age on the first day. We really hit it off with them and spent a good part of the conference with them. They had a son about our daughter's age at the time. In this marriage both the husband and the wife were physicians, and they told us about a family tradition they had back home. It involved a book for children I had written (now out of print) called *I'd Choose You!* It was about a little elephant who had a tough day. But at the end of that tough day, Norbert discovers that out of all the other kids in their city, his mom and dad would choose him every time.

This physician couple told Cindy and me that their six-year-old son loved that book. It had become a nightly ritual to read *I'd Choose You!* and tell him they loved him. That was nice to hear. What wasn't nice to hear was at breakfast the next morning when both the husband's and the wife's beepers went off at the same time. While this couple was at the conference, their young son had come down with a fever. It had shot up so high and so quickly that the babysitter became concerned and called them. They tried to help from out of state, but soon another call came. The child was being taken to the hospital. Obviously, that ended the conference for them, and they flew home as quickly as they could.

Doctors were finally able to bring the young boy's temperature down and save his life. But though he got better, the fever had robbed him of his hearing in both ears. When we heard what had happened weeks later, our hearts went out to this couple as they described how guilty they felt for not being there the day their son fell ill. How helpless they felt, even with all their medical knowledge, that they couldn't have kept him from losing his hearing.

But then we heard something else a few months later that brought tears to our eyes. With his loss of hearing, it was obvious that this couple and their son would need a way, other then spoken words, to communicate with each other. So all three of them signed up to learn sign language together. And that's when they told us, "We want to thank you for your book because it was always Danny's favorite before he lost his hearing. And when we went to the speech pathologist to learn sign language together, we told her that the first words we wanted her to teach us were *I'd choose you!* We say that to Danny every day and every night now. Hearing loss or not, he knows 'I'd choose you!'"

What a picture of genuine commitment—letting a young child know that he may have lost something valuable, his hearing, but he would never lose something of even greater worth, their love and commitment.

Personal Reflection: Did you grow up with a mother and father who said or demonstrated by their actions that no matter what, they'd choose you and be there for you? Growing up in a home with genuine commitment puts a solid floor under a child when trying times come. Do you feel like you left your home with such a stable platform for growth?

_____

_____

_____

_____

_____

Brian had read *The Blessing* when Amy was young and had done his best to do all five of those small things when she was growing up. To the best of his ability, he knew he had given her his blessing. But when she was in junior high, it still seemed that they moved miles apart. Yet do you remember what brought them together?

Connection often comes when we're doing something else together. Think about how friendships often spring up when you're working on a project with other parents from your kids' school, rooting for the same sports team, active in the same political campaign, serving together on the same ship, or assigned to the same unit. What Brian did with having Amy read to him was try to meet a need for her (reading out loud) with a small way to connect, and it worked! In the process of reading together, even though they were seldom eye to eye, they soon found their hearts being knit closer together than they had in years.

Reading a story with his child was Brian's way of doing a small thing.

2 Degree Suggestions for Parents

If you're a parent, what are some small, 2 Degree changes you could make to build a stronger relationship with a particular child? In case you need some 2 Degree suggestions that other parents have done, here's a random laundry list of such small things that might give you an idea of something small you could do to connect with your child:

1. Compliment each child once each day.
2. Never leave home without giving them a hug.
3. Point out one thing they're doing, at least once a week, that pictures a "special future."
4. Work on one puzzle for thirty minutes with your kids once a week.
5. Teach your child one chore and help him or her with that one chore.
6. Plan a ten-minute playtime with each child.
7. Make a fort with blankets in the kids' rooms or do a backyard campout one weekend night.
8. Rent a motor home and take the family on a weekend "roughing it easy" camping trip.
9. Play one board game a week with the family.
10. Read a book with your child and put that child's name in the main character's spot.
11. Take your kids to church and volunteer in their Sunday school room.
12. Read one Bible story with your child at home every Sunday evening.
13. Pray for your child(ren) and your spouse every morning when you get up and before you hit the sack.

14. Pick a family project where you can serve less fortunate people together—from a missions trip to helping at a soup kitchen or visiting an elderly person or senior adult home.

Get the picture?

Small things. The number of small things you can do to start the connection process with even a disconnected child is limitless. Start small, and perhaps this will be the one area you choose to make your 2 Degree change in when you finish each chapter.

the 2 Degree Difference lines up against a marriage that isn't working

Twenty years-plus of marriage to Jennie, and Brian felt like he was walking on black ice when it came to his relationship with his wife. After one of Brian's small-group meetings, he determined to try making 2 Degree changes in his marriage. At that small-group meeting, the men discussed Naaman the leper and his anger at being asked to do something small. Let's start this journal chapter and reflect on that story from Scripture. Here's a quote from Eric that captured the conclusion of all their sharing about this soldier's story:

> "I [Eric] think that's it for a lot of us. We've got a big problem. We need to do something big and hard to solve our problems. Asking Naaman to set aside his pride and to go wash in the Jordan seven times, when so much was at stake for him, I think seemed like nonsense. But Naaman did humble himself, and he did do that small thing that his servants said he should. And I think Naaman should be really glad that he had servants with enough guts to face him when he was angry and to tell him he was wrong. That's not easy to do with a commanding officer. But they cared for him enough to point out that maybe there was another way than just 'big problem—big solution.' Maybe small things could bring great change."

Since you've read the book, or if you've read Naaman's story in Scripture yourself, you know he was a great man with a huge problem, expecting a big solution. Thankfully, when he was ready to walk away uncured at the suggestion that he do something small, he had friends who cared enough about him not to let him walk off a cliff. Take a moment to do a "friend" survey right now. Do you have those kinds of courageous, caring friends in your life right now? Someone who would confront you if your pride or anger were motivating you to do something with long-term negative results? If so, what's a small thing you can do to say thank you to them for being there for you? If not, what's one small thing you could do to begin developing such a friend, and then after that friend, another?

_____

_____

_____

_____

Brian had such a friend in Eric and in the other men in his small group. Eric took a risk in talking to Brian about his marriage and in being persistent to meet with him and share about 2 Degree Differences. Brian also had the men in his small group rooting for him to make and follow through on 2 Degree changes in his marriage. I asked above if you had that kind of friend. Let's flip the question. Have you ever been like Naaman's friends or Eric in another person's life? If so, describe the situation you found yourself in. How did your friend respond when you confronted him or her? Was it easy or difficult for you to stand up and point out that your friend was heading toward real problems?

_____

_____

_____

_____

Even with good friends supporting him in his decision to make 2 Degree changes in his marriage, Brian had no illusions that any change would come quickly or easily. If you've got some work to do in an important relationship—your marriage, or in a relationship with someone you're seriously dating—think about this:

Would you agree that setting low expectations on the other person's response to the small things you do, along with a genuine commitment to make 2 Degree changes over time *no matter what,* is a necessary "one/two" combination? Agree or disagree and why?

_____

_____

_____

_____

_____

The great thing you have going for you when you decide to make 2 Degree changes, even in the face of a challenging marriage, is that the actions you're doing are so small that they become self-reinforcing without your having to get immediate feedback from the other person. In over a quarter of a century of working with couples, I've had literally hundreds of husbands or wives in my counseling office who have nearly (or in fact have) given up hope that anything could change. In most cases they're heartsick, as we discussed earlier. Most times you can track that back to the lack of feedback they've gotten for the things they've done for their spouse—no recognition, thanks, or positive response. Lack of affirmation lies at the heart of many who give up and walk away, convinced nothing will ever change.

Again, here's the great advantage you have in doing 2 Degree changes in your marriage. Look at the small things you do like tying your shoe. That act is so small that you don't think when you've finished tying your shoe, "Way to go! You did a great job tying your shoe." You should definitely get a "Way to tie your shoe!" from everyone in the house! While that might seem silly, that's exactly the trap many husbands and wives, particularly those who are struggling, fall into. They're so lonely or hurt or worried that things might not work out that when they do something positive, it gets infused with great expectations that something big will happen in response to what they've done.

For example, with one couple I worked with, the wife decided to divorce her husband when he didn't notice the new dress she had bought and worn just for him. She knew he loved red dresses. Personally, she wasn't a red person and did not have even one in her closet. However, she went out and got one, wore it just for him, and he said nothing.

Think back to the story of Naaman. Naaman expected Elisha himself to come out, wave his hand, and make a big deal about what was going on, particularly with so much at stake. After all, Naaman had journeyed a long way. Gone to lots of effort to get to Elijah's house. And then the man himself doesn't even come out. This woman had similar expectations of her husband—that he would notice what she'd done just for him, make a big deal about it. And like an unspoken fleece on the ground, his actions would confirm to her whether their big problems could be solved.

Of course, she never said that to her husband, but that was her thinking. I learned this after talking with both parties more than a year after their divorce. In fact, the husband had noticed the dress at the time and thought she looked awesome. But he was so worried about saying the wrong thing and hurting her feelings that he didn't say anything, thinking that would help, and yet it was his silence that convinced her that their marriage would never work out.

The great thing about making 2 Degree changes in a marriage is that it's something we should do just because it's godly! 2 Degree investments in our marriage are something anyone who is married should be doing no matter what and without expectation of praise from the other person. Look at it as just part of the work it takes to have a great relationship. And no, I'm not saying that you *shouldn't* say "thank you" or appreciate the small things a spouse does for you. You should, but God's type of love doesn't keep score.

Perhaps the most quoted, beautiful picture of God's type of love is found in 1 Corinthians 13:4–7, "Love is patient, love is kind and is not jealous; love does not brag and is not arrogant, does not act unbecomingly; it does not seek its own, is not provoked, does not take into account a wrong suffered, does not rejoice in unrighteousness, but rejoices with the truth; bears all things, believes all things, hopes all things, endures all things."

Brian had to endure a lot in doing small things with no immediate, positive feedback. But he stayed committed to doing small things, no matter what, because it is a mark of unconditional love to do small things without keeping score.

I encourage couples to get an eye dropper at their local pharmacy. Keep that on your desk or put it on the counter where you shave or put on your makeup as a "memorial marker." That's because 2 Degree changes in a marriage are like adding a single eye dropper full of water to a dry houseplant.

Adding an eye-dropper amount of water to a houseplant is not grounds for celebration. We shouldn't expect accolades, and when they don't come, we shouldn't be passive/aggressive or be secretly but obviously hurt. If you're going to keep a plant alive and even thriving, it's going to take a lot of eye droppers full of water. But they add up, one eye dropper full at a time. It's not about trying to dump a bucket of water on a plant to try and make up for what's missing. Just focus on one eye dropper a day worth of small things, done without expectation, and let the moisture of your actions begin to add life to your relationship.

Discussion Point: How easy or difficult is it for you to add those "eye-dropper" actions without getting any praise or thanks? Again, we should say thank-you to others for their positive actions, but if no thanks is forth-coming when we do something for others, how difficult is it for you to "keep adding water" to that relationship? What could help you keep going until enough moisture was added to "green" things out?

_____

_____

_____

_____

_____

Let's look now in this journal at how to pick out or see an area where you need to make a 2 Degree change in a marriage.

2°

With all the couples I work with, I always point out to them a quick and powerful way they can pinpoint areas in their marriage begging for 2 Degree changes. With those who come in for training at The Center for StrongFamilies, every one takes the Leading From Your Strengths online strengths assessment. Yes, there's a cost for the assessment, but it's an outstanding tool, and I make each couple order and pay for their own report online. I do so because people tend *not* to value things that cost them nothing. (In part, that's why I make people pay for books they are required to read as well. I realized early on that books that I just handed out sat on the shelf. Entitlement or handouts don't spur positive action as a rule.)

You can find out about the Leading From Your Strengths report at our Web site (www.the2degreedifference.com), or you can feel free to go to www.Leadingfromyourstrengths.com. Once you order a pass code, it takes each spouse only five to seven minutes to take the assessment online, and then it *instantly* e-mails back a twenty-eight-page strengths assessment! It's a powerful way for a husband or wife to see how valuable they are (it's a strengths assessment) and for this couple to see clearly where they fall on these four predictable areas of conflict. Once they can pinpoint where they are on these areas, they can begin to craft specific 2 Degree changes to help them move closer in this area and actually value each other's differences as strengths, not weaknesses.

There's no demand here that you purchase an assessment in order to understand or apply what follows. If you'll just read on, you can do a good job of highlighting where you are on these four continuums and nail down 2 Degree changes based on that information. So please don't write me letters. I teach these continuums all the time where people "get it" and act on what's shared without purchasing an assessment. However, if you can, you should do so. And again, it's not an option for any couple or individual I work with at The Center. I think it's that helpful.

With all that in mind, here's an example of the first of these four continuums that can help you in your marriage.[1]

The Forward Step/Backwards Step Lion Continuum

Are you familiar with the way pro baseball players approach different positions? By that I mean, did you know that an infielder's natural instincts are to move *in* at the crack of the bat while an outfielder's first step is usually a slight hitch or half step back as they calculate the angle they'll need to catch or cut off a ball. After all, if the ball gets behind or away from the outfielder, there's no one to back them up. They need to make decisions based on facts as much as instinct.

That's baseball. But did you know that in a marriage—or you can see this if you're a parent or even in a workplace or ministry team—you see this same thing lived out time and again when a problem or major opportunity comes up.

If someone scores high on the Lion scale on the Leading From Your Strengths report (or you can just predict where you'll score from the discussion that follows), they're like an infielder. Their God-given strength is to have that quick first step in, like a third baseman charging a ball, in order to deal with the runner quickly and throw him out. People who are low on the Lion scale are more like outfielders. Their God-given first step when a problem or "significant opportunity" comes up is a step *back*.

Let's say you've got a Step Forward/Step Backwards marriage. Can you see how this predictable area of conflict can prove problematic until each party realizes how much they need each other? You don't win baseball games if you have all infielders and no outfielders. Both strengths are valuable, and they both are strengths!

For example, if there's a small, simple, "firefighting" kind of problem, then someone with high Lion "Step Forward" strengths is a good person to put on that problem. They're comfortable with quickly jumping in and solving the problem, like dumping water on a fire. But let's say the problem is more complex. Did you know that "step forward" Lion types who try to solve a complicated problem too quickly can actually create additional problems by not having all the facts before they react? On a complex problem it's helpful to have someone with low Lion strengths. They want to go slower, think more carefully about a decision and about how best to tackle a problem.

Once a couple understands where they are on this Step Forward/Step Back dance when it comes to problems and significant opportunities, their marital satisfaction and appreciation for their spouse often dramatically goes up. They can see each other's *strengths* instead of being convinced they're just out to frustrate the other person!

For Discussion: Would you say that you primarily are a "step forward" person or a "step back" person when problems and major opportunities present themselves? You need both to have a winning team. If you're married and your spouse is at a different place from you on this continuum, how can you look at his or her strengths in a positive way as something you really need instead of as "the problem"? Again, several questions and thoughts are shared above with much to digest, so feel free to review and then write down and/or share your thoughts about this continuum:

The Words-Versus-the-Facts Otter Continuum

Another predictable area of conflict for couples is when one person is inspired to move to action by words and the other person is inspired to move only when they have the facts—and even then, only when those facts have been checked and double-checked.

This time, picture two people, one who is nearsighted and the other farsighted. If they're nearsighted, then they need help seeing far away. If they're farsighted, they struggle with "close up" vision tasks. Now think about a couple like Brian and Jennie or you and your spouse if you're married.

What happens to the average person when you put on someone else's glasses? You can't see as well, or perhaps you can't see clearly at all depending on the degree of their prescription, right? But what if you had one person who could see far away helping the one who struggled with seeing the horizon, and someone who could read well up close helping another person who struggles in that area. That's exactly what happens in the strongest marriages and is highlighted in this continuum. Only we're not talking about glasses; we're talking about what people "see" and what motivates them.

For example, some people are easily motivated by words. They are high Otters on the Leading From Your Strengths scale, and they get excited when they hear a top-notch presentation and expect everyone else to get excited when they make their own presentations. They like words, want to use many words, and rarely feel they need to slow down to read the fine print in a perspective. After all, they've seen the presentation! "What's the upside?" is often their question. Not, "What are the potential risks?"

Then you have people with low Otter strengths. These are the people who want and are motivated by facts and can even distrust too many words. In the book of Proverbs, we're told, "In an abundance of words, sin is inevitable" (10:19). Low Otters are unimpressed with many words because it comes across as unreliable, hype, sales lingo, and not serious consideration.

Can you begin to see the predictable conflict that two people at the end of each side of this continuum could have? One person, like Brian, tries using more and more words to tell Jennie that he is changed and a different person. Jennie wants Brian to skip the words and just show her the completed tasks. Facts and actions motivate for one; words motivate the other. Until they realized, talked through, and saw value in each other, this was another logjam for these two, and often for others like them.

Discussion Time: You've seen in this third continuum how words versus facts can cause real problems in a relationship if not talked through and each person's strengths valued. Where do you stand on this continuum in your marriage? What would happen if you used fewer words and more facts with a spouse who is motivated by facts by God-given strength? Or vice versa, adding words to the one who values them. Here's your chance to review this continuum and reflect on what it could say to you in your marriage and other important relationships.

$2°$

_____

_____

_____

_____

_____

_____

The Start/Finish or Golden Retriever Continuum

Perhaps the greatest logjam area for Brian and Jennie was something highlighted in the Leading From Your Strengths report that we call the Golden Retriever Continuum. We picture core personality strengths as Lions, Otters, Golden Retrievers, and Beavers. In short, people who take the report will typically score either high or low on the Golden Retriever scale. The higher they are on the Retriever scale, the more of a "finisher" they'll tend to be. If you haven't taken the report, then again, just follow the dialogue, and you'll be able to picture where you are on this continuum.

People who score very high on the Start/Finish Golden Retriever continuum, like to do one thing, and finish that one thing, and then start the next thing, and then finish the next thing. They love being able to work sequentially through issues, tasks, or projects; and they love closing loops and stamping "done" on something. That was Jennie. She was a "finisher" not only by way of her God-given strengths, but she had that "finisher" trait reinforced every day at her job as a paralegal in a large law firm. From day one her goal was not to start something she couldn't finish and to finish everything she started.

Call her Jennie the "finisher."

Then Jennie marries Brian.

Call Brian the "starter."

Brian was at the absolute bottom of the Golden Retriever scale when he took the Leading From Your Strengths report. He's the kind of person who loves to multitask and start something new all the time. Think about

Brian as a juggler (an illustration that Rodney Cox, cofounder at Leading From Your Strengths, loves to share). Brian's the kind of person who will grab one ball, then two, then three, and perhaps a fourth, and start tossing them up in the air. Lots of balls up in the air at once makes for excitement and pleases the crowd! *So what* if someone tosses another ball to Brian in the midst of all his juggling and he drops one or more of the other balls trying to catch it? Does dropping a ball or two worry or bother someone like Brian? Absolutely not! He just kicks one of the dropped balls away, picks up another, and goes back to juggling!

How do you think Jennie the "finisher" would have dealt with having a ball tossed to her from out of nowhere? In particular, how do you think she would feel if she dropped a ball or, heaven forbid, two! That would be a disaster in her thinking. If she had her choice, Jennie would juggle with only one ball at a time! It might have low theater value, but there would be a high probability that she wouldn't drop the ball.

Can you see how these two people's strengths set up a predictable area of conflict for them? To Jennie it was Brian's seemingly cavalier way of dropping and picking up balls and tasks that produced the major logjam in their relationship. And what was it that over time slowly began to break this logjam between them?

If you remember, when Brian started doing small things, their relationship began to change. Brian decided to do one "eye dropper" full of water, one small thing a day on Jennie's list.

Brian had never heard about the "Starter/Finisher Golden Retriever Continuum." He just started doing small things. Brian was doing something small each day that spoke her language. Brian would always be a three-ball juggler by choice and God-given temperament, but he was choosing to toss up one ball at a time for long enough to finish something on Jennie's chore list. Even when she, in anger, wouldn't give Brian a list or the time of day to make a list, he had eyes. Brian could look around and see things that needed to be done around the house or for her or Amy. And instead of trying to do everything at once, all he had to do was eye-dropper actions, self-reinforcing because they were so small. And again, he'd made a prior decision that his expectations would be on God causing "compound interest" growth in his time, without expectation that Jennie would say, "Thank you" or "You did a great job, Brian!" Brian was doing these small things "heartily unto the Lord," because he trusted that if he would just be faithful in the little eye dropper full of water added to his marriage each day, perhaps one day it would "green out" this relationship.

For Your Discussion: If you're married, on this Start/Finish Golden Retriever Continuum, are you at opposite ends with your spouse? Has that caused problems in the past or today? Can you see how having someone who can juggle several balls at once is actually a strength? And can you see that the person who wants only to juggle one ball at a time has important strengths as well? Keep this in mind in your marriage: Like any great team you need a starter and a finisher to complete a relay race. Both run in most marriages. The question is, how is the handoff going between the starter and the finisher?

Brian and Jennie were dropping the baton every time. But when they finally slowed down and talked and thought about it, things began to change. Brian actually started doing and finishing things that put him in her lane, and they started connecting as they had never done before. Once they figured out that this was their major logjam area, they didn't just get better in this area; their respect and value and appreciation for the other person went way up, and it helped them deal with differences in the remaining three continuums as well (that "compound interest" thing at work again).

All I've shared above is a lot to think about regarding this continuum. Take your time. Go back to the beginning of the discussion of this "Starter/Finisher" continuum and work through all the questions and observations you find above, recording your observations here below and, if possible, sharing them with your spouse if you're married.

_____

_____

_____

_____

_____

Finally, There's the Rules/Risks Beaver Continuum

One more important continuum can bring out predictable areas of conflict in a couple or in other teams. That's when you have one person who prefers and is very rule oriented and another closely related who is a risk taker. The high Beaver strengths person is typically very rule conscious. They see safety in rules and standard procedures. They feel there is stability and predictability in knowing how others have done something and following a set way of doing things. As you might imagine, they often marry someone who is a low Beaver risk taker. They don't look for precedent; they look for fresh snow. In other words, they don't have to stay on the wide, groomed trail but can see something exciting through the trees and take off and make a new trail of their own! Again, both are God-given strengths. Both are valuable to a team or ministry or family or marriage. But you simply must talk through and learn to value and appreciate these differences if you're to avoid the logjam that Brian and Jennie faced.

Once again, why were Brian's 2 Degree changes, even when they weren't talking to each other very much, so helpful? When he decided to finish one small thing a day, he was doing something that helped them draw closer in this continuum as well without even knowing it. All Brian knew was that he was going to add that eye dropper full of water to his marriage. That's my challenge to you as you talk about this continuum and if you decide to make 2 Degree changes in your marriage. Just do it. Just do small things, even if you don't understand all the psychological, emotional, spiritual underpinnings that attach to the 2 Degree changes you're making.

For Discussion: Is this fourth continuum, Rules/Risks, something you need to talk about as a couple? Which of the four above do you feel provides the greatest potential logjam in your marriage? Which one(s) are you close to each other on already?

2°

Closing Thoughts in This Journal Chapter

There's a great deal of material for thought already in this section. I'll just close with a few final thoughts and then a list of suggestions if you're still not sure what a 2 Degree action might be in a marriage.

First, do you remember the small changes Brian started adding to his marriage? Setting his watch to beep at 3:00 p.m. Doing one thing a day on a chore chart, even if he had to make up his own chore chart. And he cut out a small, one-inch square of cloth to remind him to do that one thing. That's not a lot, but over time it did a lot.

But do you remember the small thing that tipped things for this couple? It was when he started opening the car door for her. Keep in mind: actions dictate feelings, not the reverse. Brian would have waited forever for Jennie to wake up and feel valued with the words he used. His actions actually woke her up to the fact that she still had feeling for him.

Here's that list of small, 2 Degree actions that other couples have made:

1. Keep plastic mistletoe hung in your home year-round.
2. Warm your spouse's towel in the dryer before he or she gets out of the shower or bath.
3. Celebrate the anniversary of when you first met.
4. Celebrate your spouse's half-birthday each year.
5. Have a card or sign waiting for them when they get back from a trip telling them you missed them.
6. Write them a note for their lunch box or slip it in the cup holder of their car.
7. Ask your spouse three questions about their day when you walk in the door.
8. Leave a love note in a book they're reading.
9. Rent a movie they like and watch it with them.
10. Window-shop together.
11. Make a call from work or school to check on them.
12. Take a walk together.
13. Squeeze their hand three times as a way of saying, "I love you."
14. Open the door for your wife.

15. Compliment your husband in public.
16. Say, "I'm sorry."
17. Give the kids a bath.
18. Finish one chore.

These are just a few of the countless ways you can make an eye-dropper deposit of warm, love, value, and blessing into your spouse's life, a *2 Degree Difference*.

Notes

1. You can also see diagrams of what you see in the assessment and other suggestions in *HeartShift* regarding making 2 Degree changes in a marriage.

the 2 Degree Difference and the incredible shrinking belt

These next three journal chapters will be shorter because in both the area of health and fitness and in the workplace, there are many outstanding books and Web sites that can give you lots of the theory and background on why small changes can change so much in these areas. My training has come in working with people, so I'll make fewer written suggestions on the process of change in our health and in the workplace and refer you to several excellent resources from experts who advocate making small steps in those two areas. In the next several journal chapters, we'll focus on capturing thoughts, sharing key concepts, and looking closely at what you personally can do to make a *2 Degree Difference* in your health first of all and then in your workplace.

Brian's wake-up call in the health area came when his doctor told him to lose weight and get in shape "or else." Looking at your health history, has there been an "or else" meeting between you and a doctor or surgeon? If so, did it motivate you? And if so, for how long? Describe the circumstances and situation. If you've never had a medical wake-up call, what has been your primary motivation to get or stay in shape?

2°

_____

_____

Brian went to a Web site he heard about on the radio, www.small step.gov. If that mention of the Web site by Brian hasn't already prompted you to go online, then I urge you to visit this site on health and small steps. It has a section for adults and an excellent section for children, encouraging them to take small health steps as well. It's a great place, among many on the Web, to find cutting-edge suggestions on health and fitness.

After you have gone to the site, what is one thing you found there that you felt might actually be a practical or helpful small step you could take in your health?

_____

_____

_____

_____

_____

_____

Brian tried several big steps toward getting in shape. None worked. What has been your experience when it comes to exercise? Is it something you've found relatively easy to build into your life, or is exercise something that comes along about as often as Halley's comet?

_____

_____

_____

_____

Brian came face-to-face with an old high school football teammate. If you remember, this same person also made him feel terrible with his "swallowed the football" joke. Have you ever been the brunt of jokes about your size or health? Has that motivated you to do something in the past—long-term, short-term, or not at all? Explain your answer.

_____

_____

_____

_____

Brian picked as one of his first 2 Degree changes to eat "one salad a day." How realistic would that be for you in your work, school, or home situation? Would that be too big of a first step for you—a salad every day? Explain your answer.

_____

_____

_____

_____

How small a first step can you make and still have it be meaningful?

I get asked that question often when we're training people or I'm teaching this concept to groups. Here's an example of how small is too small.

Two years ago at the time of this writing, I spoke at one of our family's favorite family camps, Pine Cove in Tyler, Texas. A man sat in the back every session. He was friendly, quiet, and extremely overweight. While we said hello and chatted briefly, we never had a long talk, and I didn't know what, if anything, he might be taking home after learning about the *2 Degree Difference.*

I found out what he had been thinking and planning when a letter arrived at my home one year later, complete with a before and after picture. What this man had decided to do was to go home and start cutting down on his food intake by going from two desserts a night to one. You read that correctly. Two desserts to one was his small, 2 Degree health change at the beginning. Was he serious? Inside the envelope were the before and after shots of two very different people and this letter:

> *Dear Dr. Trent,*
>
> *Thanks for your talks last year on the 2 Degree change. That principle was crucial in my having lost well over 100 lbs in the past year. Starting is often the most difficult part of weight loss, and I found that the concept of just a 2 Degree change in my behavior really enabled me to be patient, until I began to see actual results. Of course, the Lord was the true engine of change for me, but you and your ministry played a crucial part. I would love to tell you more, like for instance that I ran a full marathon in February!*
>
> *Sincerely,*
>
> *Troy*

The problem this man always faced before was setting "way out there" diet and exercise goals (like Brian) and then getting discouraged and quitting before there was any obvious change. But something different happened when he went small by going from two desserts to one. That gave him enough confidence to go from one dessert a night to one every other night. Then one every third night. And he approached exercise the same way. Small steps at first. Then longer walks. Then walking and jogging. And then jogging and walking. And now he's run the Marine Corps Marathon in Washington, DC, (his first ever) and has lost more than one hundred pounds and kept it off! In fact, Mark was the star of the advertising campaign for the book *HeartShift!*

I love his story because it goes to the heart of "How small is too small?" In your health, it can be as small as two desserts to one. But keep in mind, Mark was serious about losing weight. It wasn't a joke like, "I'm cutting down from three dozen Krispy Kreme chocolate cream donuts to two." He, like Brian, was serious about losing weight. Both of them had legitimate health issues staring them in the face if they didn't lose weight. And with young children and a wife whom he loved very much depending on him to be around for a while, he was serious about applying the *2 Degree Difference* to his health. But he also was wise enough after hearing me talk to go slow—real slow in his case! But slow enough and small enough steps that he actually felt like he was gaining ground—until he actually started losing weight. The larger steps he made came from lots and lots of small steps that were self-reinforcing.

For Discussion: What do you think about the "How small is too small" discussion above? If you were serious about making one small step to improve your health, what would it be? Why?

_____

_____

_____

I've already mentioned www.smallstep.gov as a good Internet starting point. Let me recommend a book as well (or actually now a series of books) that is good on starting small with diet and exercise goals. I like *8 Minutes in the Morning: A Simple Way to Shed Up to 2 Pounds a Week Guaranteed* by Jorge Cruise. It's a book on why small steps in our health can carve out big health benefits. There are many others, but just start with the small step of your own that you outlined above. Even if it's "cut down to one soda and one small bag of chips a day" and you've been at "four sixty-four-ounce sodas and a pound of chips a day." If you're serious, small things can mean everything in moving you toward better health.

the 2 Degree Difference attacks a stacked deck at work and the 2 Degree Difference and cold-calling on a new career

You've noticed, I'm sure, that I'm combining two chapters into one in this journal chapter. That's because they both draw on the workplace as a place where many of us can help shape our lives and careers by making 2 Degree changes. I'll list some business books for reference (of which there are many) where you can get all the theory and business application you want on making small changes in the workplace. In these combined journal chapters we'll focus on what the *2 Degree Difference* meant to Brian in his job and what it can mean to you and your career and everyday workplace success as well.

Chapter 12 begins with Brian finally seeing movement with his wife. This discussion of his marriage in the business section of the book was done for a reason. It's because the way things are going, good or bad, in your family makes a tremendous difference in everything you do in business and at work. Here's an example that surprised Cindy and me.

Several years ago, right after Desert Storm, we received a call at my office from the United States Army. It was a psychologist, stationed at the time in Germany, and he wanted us to come overseas and help a certain group of troops with something important. We did go, and we had the honor of meeting, coaching, encouraging, and training some of our elite troops and their spouses in how to have stronger families.

What in the world would the army be doing bringing over stateside resources to help rangers and airborne troops with their *families?* How did that fit with their mission and purpose? Actually, what prompted the call was a study they had done on combat readiness before the shooting war in Kuwait broke out.

Guess what was the main deterrent to combat readiness for these best of the best, tip of the spear troops? Was it conditioning? Absolutely not. They were in incredible physical shape. Was it training or equipment? They were among the best-trained, best-outfitted fighting units in the world. Morale? Outstanding. What then was kicking the slats out from under them emotionally and was listed as the main reason for not being ready for combat? Poor family relationships.

I share that because so much of business and work is like going to war. Obviously, most of us don't actually put our lives on the line. But there are many parallels between business and going out to do battle. The business world is challenging, demanding, relentless, and at times scary. And yet, if you have a strong family behind you, it's amazing how much it frees you to look forward, face challenges, overcome obstacles—all that when you don't have to worry about what awaits you when you get back.

That's the reason in chapter 12 on the workplace, you have a long section on Brian and his wife. Home and the workplace are absolutely interrelated. People often look at a top executive who tosses aside the wife of his youth for a younger version, and they may think he (and she) is too rich to worry about a broken relationship. As someone who has counseled with many such people, that's absolutely not true. It eats their lunch when they're alone, and when they get older, and when their children tell them not to come to their wedding, and when the new younger wife leaves them for someone younger and richer. Poor family relationships cripple even the most successful business people.

It has been my honor to be acquainted with some of the most successful businesspeople in the world. In one training university overseas, the entire group Cindy and I taught had last names that were "brand names" you'd find on the shelf of Home Depot or any clothing store. Here were world leaders in business with their families learning ways to strengthen their home. Poor family relationships aren't just the main factor in bringing down combat readiness. It's the main factor in pulling us down in whatever workplace setting we're in.

With all that in mind, how have you seen your family relationships factor in good or in challenging ways to your attention, energy, creativity, and interest at work?

_____

_____

_____

_____

_____

The day came when Brian was called down to Mr. Crowley's office. Brian had already started making 2 Degree changes at work. It started with his decision not to use a derogatory nickname for Mr. Crowley. Let's stay with that for a moment. How serious is it to place a negative nickname or label on someone we work with or for?

_____

_____

_____

_____

Brian was handed a pink slip one day. He did get a severance package. He did get handed the paper personally by his boss. But after nearly two decades at the job, you'd think one of the owners or a whole group of people would have surrounded Brian with pats on the back and a "job well done." But that's too often a picture of yesterday, not today. Today we get let go via e-mail as I did recently. For eight years I had the privilege of writing a regular column in a magazine, article after article for ninety-six months on being a godly father. I lasted through three different editors in that time frame. And then, when the magazine went through yet another iteration and update, I got an e-mail from the new editor saying, "We don't need your column anymore. Thanks!" I sent back an e-mail asking if after eight years someone should at least call and fire me. I received back another nice e-mail saying that she was sorry, and busy, and I was right. They should have been more sensitive, but after all, e-mail is so *convenient* today. Eight years and I never did then or since receive a call from anyone.

That's not whining. That's the norm today. There is simply no institutional memory of what you did, the sacrifices or tasks you took on, the miles you logged like Brian.

What about you? Have you been unceremoniously let go at a job or task? What did that do to your emotions? To your sense of being valuable? How motivated were you to head out the next day and look for something new?

_____

_____

_____

_____

_____

Before Brian was let go, he decided to take the "one-inch frame" idea from the coffee shop and small group to his workplace. He started making one callback every time he sat down at his desk. This way he would complete just one task he normally put off. Sit down and make *one* call. Even if it was to a supplier you knew was going to blame you for something that happened on an order that you didn't take. Yet that small step started a follow-through process that helped Brian in the many tasks he had as a traveling salesperson.

Discussion Time: For Brian it was a small frame and the commitment to do two, small, specific, positive things at work: call "The Bulldog" by his real name, Mr. Crowley, and make one "least favorite" phone call every time he sat down at his desk. What are one or two small, specific, positive 2 Degree changes you could make in your workplace?

Potential first step, small steps at *your* workplace: _____

_____

———————————————————

———————————————————

———————————————————

———————————————————

I mentioned that there were a number of good business books that link "small things" with great gains in the workplace. The most recent is one I mentioned earlier—*Broken Windows, Broken Business: How the Smallest Remedies Reap the Biggest Rewards.* That's just the most current at this time of writing. Walk the shelves in the business management section of your bookstore, and you'll see one after another book stressing the small things that can mean everything to customer loyalty, brand building, quality, delivery of services, and the bottom line. If you haven't read it yet, Giuliani's outstanding book, *Leadership,* is well worth reading. Whether you are running the nation's largest city or the newest "worker bee" at a start-up business, small things can help you move from where you are today to standing next to your goals tomorrow.

2⁰

fast-forward: a life of purpose at last lived out

wish I could push past the horizon and see the exciting, hopeful things God has laid out for your future. If I could, then I could come up with a series of questions about how your life-story gains were tied to the small changes you made. Instead, let's close our journal process by looking at our friend Brian. Cycle back through the short conclusion in chapter 14. While some are subtle, make a list of the different areas where "small things" began to change everything for Brian more than a year down the road from that wake-up-call plane trip.

What changed or was changing for Brian in the time since he woke up on the plane and woke up on the day of his race?

_____

_____

_____

_____

_____

If you think about it, a great many loops closed; new habits were established; and emotional, relational, and spiritual gains were made. And here's the amazing thing: once you get to a place where you're moving forward, did you realize it takes far less energy to keep moving than it does to get things started?

2°

From the Lockheed Martin Web site, you can discover that the builders of the space shuttle need to generate one million pounds of thrust to get the shuttle off the ground and into orbit. Yet it takes only a miniscule amount of energy once the ship gets up and moving to send it on its mission and bring it home. You don't need huge engines to get the shuttle home; you need huge engines to get it started and moving through the atmosphere that initially holds the spacecraft back. The same thing is true with a train. It takes tremendous energy to get the train moving, and yet once it reaches speed, it can draw on less energy once the weight of the train is in motion.

It's your turn now to start moving toward your goals. And no, you don't need to manufacture one million pounds of thrust. Like putting a car in low gear, which has the most traction but is able to go the slowest speed, it's not about a racing start. It's about a 2 Degree start. How about opening the car door for your spouse? Returning one call that's a challenge to make? Walking around one block? Making good eye contact with your child when you pick her up from school? Hugging your son before you let him get out the door?

For what probably seems like the hundredth time and the last time, it's not the big things that can do the most for you in days to come. I believe that with all my heart. It's not committing to read through the Bible three times this year. It's reading one paragraph a day. It's not losing sixty pounds in the month before your reunion. It's cutting down from two deserts to one and showing up at the next reunion with your marathon medal.

In Part II and Part III of the Journal, you'll find a work sheet to write down your first 2 Degree goals and steps starting with just one area. You'll find additional pages that help you capture additional thoughts and ideas, Web sites and books that support this idea of doing small things, note pages for recording insights from the *HeartShift* book, successes and struggles, and questions you still want to ask your small group or continue to research and pray over.

Most of all, because you've come this far, I also truly believe that Almighty God has some great things in store for you. Things you couldn't have imagined would happen will happen because you know about *2 Degree Differences* and how small things can change everything.

Part III

Your 2 Degree Plan of Action

Having finished the journal and made a commitment to begin the process of living out 2 Degree changes, the following work sheet can be used as an accountability prayer and sharing sheet. As you may have more than one area where you decide you want to make a 2 Degree change, we've provided several sheets for you to complete. As you add areas, you have our permission to copy this personal goal work sheet if needed.

Brian had three areas where he launched his "small step" plan. First, he started reading with his daughter in the car. Second, in his marriage, he had two small, specific, positive 2 Degree changes he committed to make. Praying for his wife at 3:00 p.m. when his alarm watch beeped and doing one chore each day on her list, even if he had to guess at her list. Similar to the alarm watch, he reminded himself about doing one chore a day by cutting a one-inch piece of cloth and putting it in his wallet right next to his coffee card.

If you're working through this journal with a small group, then many people find it helpful to make a photocopy of their goal sheet and give it to others who are supporting and praying for them. This work sheet is just one way to help you keep track of your commitment to make small changes in a specific area. If you're artistic, or want to create something on your own that you can blow up or shrink down or hole-punch or staple to something, feel free to customize this sheet so that it's most helpful to you.

2°

My 2 Degree Change Commitment Sheet

Date: _____

The area I've picked for my 2 Degree change is: _____
_____
_____
_____

The small, specific, positive action(s) I'm going to undertake and trust will grow at "compound interest" is (are):

_____
_____
_____
_____

Someone who will be praying, helping, and/or lovingly holding me accountable to this commitment to doing small things is:

_____
_____
_____
_____

240 THE 2 DEGREE DIFFERENCE

My 2 Degree Change Commitment Sheet

Date: _____

The area I've picked for my 2 Degree change is: _____

_____

_____

_____

The small, specific, positive action(s) I'm going to undertake and trust will grow at "compound interest" is (are):

_____

_____

_____

_____

_____

Someone who will be praying, helping, and/or lovingly holding me accountable to this commitment to doing small things is:

_____

_____

_____

_____

_____

2°

My 2 Degree Change Commitment Sheet

Date: _____

The area I've picked for my 2 Degree change is: _____

_____

_____

_____

The small, specific, positive action(s) I'm going to undertake and trust will grow at "compound interest" is (are):

_____

_____

_____

_____

_____

Someone who will be praying, helping, and/or lovingly holding me accountable to this commitment to doing small things is:

_____

_____

_____

_____

_____

My *2 Degree Difference*
Notes and Observation Pages

Related ways I've seen the idea of making "small steps" presented around me, from studies of Scripture to the HeartShift book to other books and Web sites.